The Complete Guide to

PROPERTY STRATEGIES

Angela Bryant

The Complete Guide to Property Strategies

First published in 2018 by

Panoma Press Ltd
48 St Vincent Drive, St Albans, Herts, AL1 5SJ, UK
info@panomapress.com
www.panomapress.com

Book layout by Neil Coe.

Printed on acid-free paper from managed forests.

ISBN 978-1-784521-37-0

Printed and bound in Great Britain by TJ International Ltd, Padstow, Cornwall

Dedication

I dedicate this book to my children, Sophie, Chris and Matt.

Disclaimer

Although the author and publisher have made every effort to ensure that the information contained in this book was correct at the time of press, the author and publisher do not assume and hereby disclaim any liability to any party for loss, damage or disruption caused by errors or omissions, whether resulting from negligence, accident, or any other cause.

The book is intended for general guidance only and does not constitute mortgage, accountancy, financial, tax, or any other professional advice, for which you should always seek professional advice individually tailored to your circumstances and needs.

Please note that your own individual circumstances will vary uniquely from the general examples and guidance given and that Angela Bryant does not accept any responsibility or liability for loss which may arise from sole reliance on the information contained in this book.

This book covers the UK property market, including regulations, finance and taxation matters which will not apply elsewhere.

Acknowledgements and Thanks

I would like to thank my husband David Bryant, my partner in business as well as in life. My hero. My rock. Without whom our success would not be possible.

I would also like to thank all those who have cajoled, inspired and influenced me. Especial thanks to Richard Bowser of Property Investor News, for first suggesting I do the work of writing this book!

With special thanks to those interviewed for the book, including Davin and Atuksha Poonwassie of Simple Crowdfunding; Glenn Ackroyd, one of the founding directors of EweMove and former director of A Quick Sale Ltd; and Ryan Carruthers, one to watch. Also to Brendan Quinn, John Corey and others for hosting great events with inspiring speakers including some amazing developers, from whom I have learned so much.

Also to Mindy Gibbins-Klein and the team at Panoma Press for all your support.

With best wishes to all for your good fortune.

Summary of Chapters

Contents

Chapter 9: CROWDFUNDING 175

INTRODUCTION

*"Become the chess player.
Stop being the chess piece."*

Tony Robbins

Times have changed since I wrote my first book, *The Complete Guide to Property Investing Success*, yet it is still possible, starting today, to build a successful business in property. In this book I will introduce many successful people, including some who started in property in only recent years. I have researched and investigated what strategies are working best today to help you build a successful business, whether you are starting out, adapting to survive, or simply looking for new ideas.

I hope you will enjoy learning what steps I am personally taking, as well as hearing from other amazing investors. In property, there is no one size fits all. We each form our own unique success from the myriad of variables to be considered. I call this the kaleidoscope approach, which I will explain in Chapter 1 on Strategic Planning.

We are living in times of rapid and tumultuous change, none more so it seems than in property. However, before we look at the challenges investors face today, let's remind ourselves of the upside.

There are still many great reasons for investing in property:

- The private rented sector is a significant and growing part of the housing market;

- Property prices are rising by around 5% a year;

- Values doubling historically between 7-12 years with around 15 years expected in future;

- Gross rental yields additionally provide income at an average rate of 6%;

- Property provides far greater returns than savings and is far more stable than investing in shares;

- You can borrow up to 75 % so leveraging your gains;

- And there are no limits to the number of properties you can buy.

This book covers a wide variety of strategies for making money from property, with the aim of helping you decide the best way forward, whether you are a beginner, looking to change up a gear, or are having to adapt your business due to outside forces including government pressure on buy-to-let in recent years.

While some strategies are generally considered lower budget than others, this can vary down to a case-by-case level. You can grow with your business whatever your budget, depending on your own resourcefulness and knowledge, which this book will help to provide you with.

We will explore the many ways in which you can get involved in property and step-up to greater levels of success, despite the many challenges investors face today with taxation, legislation and finance – all of which will be addressed.

After the first chapter which is devoted to strategic planning, the book moves on to consider the various strategies, before dealing with finance and tax. You may want to read the whole book through first, or if a particular chapter appeals and strikes you as most interesting, jump straight to it. Aim to learn as much as you can both about traditional buy-to-let and the wide variety of other ways to make money through property.

When I wrote *The Complete Guide to Property Investing Success*, it was simply a case of explaining the great returns available from buy-to-let and inviting all to join the party. Since then, property investing has become more complicated, in part due to a natural maturing and sophistication of the market, in part as a response to outside pressures.

The financial crisis that hit from the end of 2008 led to recession, prices falling and lenders retreating from the market. This caused difficulties for many investors, particularly developers and landlords in hard-hit areas.

Since then and over the course of the last few years, the government has sought to rein in buy-to-let with increasing tax and legislation. It is more important than ever to be fully aware of the latest changes; to be ready and willing to adapt; to be flexible in assessing chosen strategies – to be strategic. The aim of this book is to show you how.

The main constraints, each of which will be discussed in more detail later, include: The removal of tax relief on mortgage interest for higher-rate taxpayers, being phased in from the tax year ended April 2017 to 2020. (Often referred to as 'Section 24', 'S24', or Clause 24 – given it is Section 24 of the Finance (no. 2) Act 2015). Note that you will only be affected if you are or will be a higher-rate tax payer and have mortgages.

- A 3 % stamp duty surcharge on 'additional properties', applying from April 2016.

- Tighter rules for lending to larger-scale investors, from October 2017, dictated by the Prudential Regulation Authority (PRA);

- Greater regulation. It is more important than ever to join a professional landlords' organisation such as the National Landlords Association (NLA) or the Residential Landlords Association (RLA). Both are excellent at keeping us informed on matters such as regulations.

- Local councils are responsible for implementing many of the national regulations and can have powers to make some variations, so always be sure to liaise with your local council about their requirements.

- What's next? The Conservative government is considering plans to require all landlords to register with a property ombudsman scheme.

- The current Labour leader has said he would introduce rent controls.

With all these pressures on our business, property is certainly not for the faint-hearted. Before you let it put you off, however, it is important to emphasise that these measures have been introduced for the very reason that property investing is SO attractive – that's why the government sees the need to 'cool the market'.

There is no doubt that the UK has a housing crisis as there are not enough homes being built for the growing population. This has led to the political will to make as many homes as possible available to first-time buyers, while investors are seen as competing. However, this political stance doesn't take into account that investors often house people who would otherwise not be able to buy or want to buy. The truth is that basically the country needs to build more homes – and as investors, we would do well to get involved in that too, through development!

Nevertheless, the private rented sector (PRS) is an important segment of the property market and is inherently linked to the UK economy. The government knows this and therefore does support the housing market – through lowering interest rates for example, to help avoid a crash. As investors we should remain calm and take steps to safeguard ourselves from measures that are designed to *rein in* the market, while not losing sight of the fact that property continues to be a brilliant investment.

As I am among the key target group most affected by the removal of mortgage interest relief for higher-rate taxpayers, I have taken steps to offset the effects, by selling some of our properties to reduce our mortgage debt. The capital gains released through selling has enabled us to help our children, as well as reducing our mortgage debt from over 75% to 50% of the properties' value. It has given us the opportunity to cull the worst performing properties in the portfolio, thus improving the overall quality, and to get involved in other areas such as property development.

It's a case of: *"When life hands you lemons – make lemonade!"*

I am excited about the future and invite readers to come with me on this journey, as we consider the wide variety of strategies that are available to be adopted in property today.

Over the past 20 years I have engaged in a number of activities within property, so I aim to add value to each strategy by mentioning my own experiences where appropriate, including:

- Straightforward buy-to-let, being my main strategy;

- Development projects: I give details of the projects I have been involved in;

- Managing properties for others;

- Being a franchisee of a property group;

- Sourcing property to buy below market value;

- Renting to a variety of tenant types, from benefits to rent-to-buy tenants;

- HMOs;

- Sale and rent back (when it was permitted);

- Buying and selling at auction;

- Lease options;

- Bridging;

- Professional training undertaken for property management;

- Crowdfunding, as an investor;

- Training investors; as well as mentoring;

- And writing property books!

Many long-term investors try various things over time. A flow in some or other direction may become your main focus either permanently or for a while, or you might return to your main activity. When trying new things, it's best not to overdo it: normally 80% of your resources should remain in the area of business that is already working for you. The 80/20 principle is well known and applies to any business. You may temporarily devote more time and attention to a new strategy, but should never redirect more than 10-20% of available funds to anything that remains as yet unproven.

While I myself have begun to look at various other strategies, standard buy-to-let still remains our main business and is, I believe, at the core of property investing. Many other strategies in property are variants, dependent on the core fact that renting out property provides an income and is what makes property investing viable. It is fundamentally the ability of property to produce an income as well as capital gains which makes it an attractive asset – whether the specific aim is buy-to-let or to sell on.

Standard buy-to-let is straightforward and has just two basic features:

1. **Positive net income:** Income must be produced from the property to support any borrowing and provide profit; positive cashflow comes from keeping expenses below the income level.

2. **Capital gains:** bought well, in a decent location, medium-to-long-term, property should yield not only rental income but great capital gains.

Whether you are starting out in property or already immersed, it is more important than ever to have a good grasp of the history of property investing. Let's now take a look at the past, present and future of property:

The Past

Twenty-five years ago, before the advent of buy-to-let mortgages, landlords numbered in the tens of thousands. Before 1996, property investing was the preserve of those rich enough to buy for cash or able to secure commercial funding, difficult for most to get.

The Housing Act of 1988 saw the introduction of the Assured Shorthold Tenancy which gave potential landlords and lenders confidence that tenants would only reside in the property for a fixed period. This led in 1996 to the birth of the buy-to-let mortgage, making it far easier for many would-be landlords to invest as they only had to save a deposit and could borrow the rest of the money required to purchase a rental property.

Property investing became popular in 1996 with the advent of buy-to-let mortgages, which is more or less when I began investing.

The Council of Mortgage Lenders reported in 2015 that lenders have advanced more than 1.7 million buy-to-let loans between 1999 and 2015. Over this time, the private rented sector doubled in size. "Buy-to-let mortgage balances outstanding recently grew to more than £200 billion" they reported.

Over the last 25 years, the private rented sector has grown significantly, in contrast to social housing, and the percentage of owner-occupiers has also decreased. The private rented sector is thus now a significant part of the housing market, providing homes to millions of people in the UK.

Over the long term, UK property has doubled in value on average every 7-12 years.

It is such rising values – or capital appreciation – that many investors regard as the big prize which property holds, while also providing rental income of course, some arguing that this *yield* is the main thing you should rely on.

The Present

Today almost two million private landlords own 4.9 million properties according to a report by Paragon Mortgages, one of the UK's biggest buy-to-let lenders, who estimate that around one in five homes in the UK are now owned by private landlords.

The Land Registry House Price Index latest report from 2017 shows an annual increase in property values of 5.6% which takes the average in the UK to £220,094. England saw an increase of 5.7% taking the average price to £236,519.

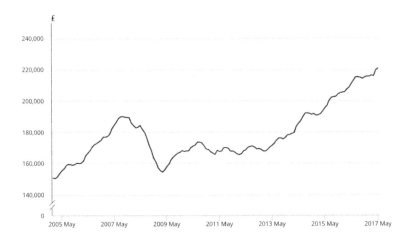

Figure 1: Average UK house price, January 2005 to May 2017

Source: HM Land Registry

Latest figures from Paragon Mortgages (April 2017) indicate the average gross rental return (gross yield) for landlords is 6%, in line with the long-term average since 2005. While 64% of landlords reported yields between 4-7%, 22% were doing better with almost one in ten (9%) reporting gross yields above 10%. The gross rental yield can be found by dividing the annual rent by the property value.

How to find the gross yield:

Rent: £1,200 per calendar month

Property value (or price): £230,000

Gross yield: £1,200 x 12 = £14,400 / £230,000 = 0.062 x 100 = 6%

Furthermore, you can normally borrow up to 75% to purchase properties (assuming you are eligible for a buy-to-let mortgage) either in a limited company or in your own name. This leverage enables you to multiply the benefit of rising property values.

Summary of Some Current Market Statistics:

- Average UK house prices: £236,519 (Land Reg, April 2017)

- Average rental yields: 6% (Paragon Mortgages, April 2017)

- Size of the PRS: 4.9 million properties, one in five homes (Paragon)

- There are now 2.5 million more households in the PRS than there were in 2000

- Younger households are now more likely to rent than to own a home

- 60% of landlords own just one property (CML report)

- Just 7% of landlords own five or more, but these account for nearly 40% of the total (CML report)

The Future

It is widely predicted that this historical rate of growth is likely to slow down, but experts still think that house prices could double by 2030, within 14 years.

The shortage of supply remains a crucial factor in keeping prices rising, together with not enough house building to meet demand. The historically cheap mortgage rates further underpin prices, and are still at record lows despite the recent rise in interest rates.

On the other hand, affordability continues to be stretched due to low wage growth, while at the higher end of the market owners are less likely to move due to the excessive cost of stamp duty.

I hope this introduction has truly set the scene of the property market now and opportunities that still exist despite the challenges investors face. Now that we have laid the groundwork, let's begin to build on your property success, with some strategic planning.

Further Reading, Resources and References

Book: *The Complete Guide to Property Investing Success* by Angela Bryant, (Ecademy Press, 2008)

Land Registry House Price Index: https://www.gov.uk/government/news/uk-house-price-index-hpi-for-april-2017

Council of Mortgage Lenders Report: https://www.cml.org.uk/news/news-and-views/buy-to-let-the-past-is-no-guide-to-the-future/

The Paragon Mortgages PRS Report 2015 can be found at www.paragon-mortgages.co.uk

House price predictions from Rightmove for 2018: http://www.rightmove.co.uk/news/house-price-index/

UK House Price Index: May 2017: https://www.ons.gov.uk/economy/inflationandpriceindices/bulletins/housepriceindex/may2017

CHAPTER 1

STRATEGIC PLANNING

"It is not the strongest of the species that survive, nor the most intelligent, but those most adaptable to change."

Charles Darwin (1809 – 1882)

Clarity: knowledge: action: You need to develop clarity about what you want first, then absorb relevant knowledge, before creating a strategic plan of action.

This chapter will set the scene for the rest of the book, by helping you consider how to go about this strategic planning.

The Cambridge dictionary describes strategy as *"a detailed plan for achieving success in situations such as war, politics, business, industry or sport, or the skill of planning such situations"*. A detailed plan may seem complicated, but when building a business, we map out a broad plan then fill in the details over time. Step by step, anything is achievable.

Big, worthwhile plans do not generally happen instantly, although people can fall in love with ideas such as building a successful portfolio. This big picture idea is your **vision** and is a very good place to start.

So how do you develop clarity of your vision? By assimilating all the possibilities, elements and factors then choosing what you want and need to include. You may have heard the saying: *"When the student is ready, the teacher will appear."* You might in this instance say: *"When the student is ready, the **vision** will appear!"*

The planning process is circular and selective, rather like creating an attractive kaleidoscope image.

The Kaleidoscope

A kaleidoscope was a much-loved toy in many homes when I was growing up, including ours. There was endless fascination to be found in the myriad patterns produced and reconfigured with every twist and turn, the pieces inside creating patterns of many colours and hues, all shapes and sizes. The pieces in the kaleidoscope could even in some cases be changed. For any given pattern, some pieces might not be in the view hence becoming irrelevant, while other pieces might overlap creating yet more variations. Some patterns turned out quite small or minimalist, others busy and full.

Given the image is formed by considering what's in view of the relevant segment, it could also be described in terms of 'what's on your radar'. A whole range or orbit of possibilities exists, but you choose only to be concerned with those in the segment of your choice: what's included in your vision.

Each person can create a unique and stunning vision for their business and life. You choose what is most appealing to you, what suits you. We must create our ideal vision before setting goals to achieve the mission of getting what we want. That is not to say it's easy or that it will necessarily come about just as planned, but the vision leads to the mission and hopefully to fruition!

As with a kaleidoscope, things can change and shift, whether or not of our choosing. In reality, nothing is fixed, and we must be capable of adapting to change. Do what you can to maintain a stable picture. Stick to your vision. The book *The Millionaire Next Door* by Thomas J Stanley, emphasised that millionaires are on the whole a stable bunch, not prone to whimsical change.

However, there are times when change is thrust upon us – like when the government suddenly changes the rules. When the picture is changed by such outside forces, when we are nudged, we may wish things could stay the same, but we must accept change and set a new vision. Who knows, it may even be a better one, so onwards and upwards!

Each of the pieces within the kaleidoscope that help to make up the overall picture can be likened to the various elements that make up our businesses. Similarly, for each strategy looked at throughout this book, you will be able to weigh it up, consider the merits, the problems and issues, risks, scalability and potential combinations, to arrive at a formula that you consider best for your own business. This is strategic planning.

The kaleidoscope is also about the idea that no one size fits all and there's no one right answer. Each person, each business is unique, like the patterns in a kaleidoscope.

Remember that you don't have to create a full and busy vision. You can keep it simple. Your vision may be simple yet elegant and still unique. 60% of landlords own just one property. Perhaps your vision is of just one bright dot, right on target!

My son Matt thought it would be better to keep it simple and produced these *circle of influence* charts for me, as an alternative to the kaleidoscope images I had planned. They are similar in effect to a pie chart, but without specifying percentages in a fixed way. Whatever floats your boat! It's about finding ways that inspire you to organise your thoughts regarding new strategies.

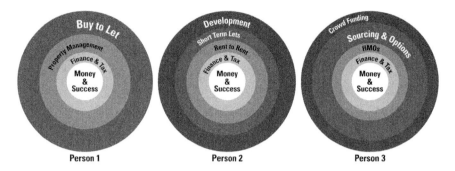

Do not allow yourself to get overwhelmed, as that is counter-productive to success. Do only what you can, starting from where you are. Focus is more valuable and productive than trying to do too much.

Sometimes the things you don't do can be as much a part of your success as what you do! It can be better to choose NOT to do something – or not now. There is a right time and a wrong time. In terms of the market cycle, timing is important. Everything has an opportunity cost too, so don't overload yourself by trying what is not right for you. Do only what suits you and let your vision be your guide.

As well as which property strategies to adopt, it's important to consider such elements as:

- You, your personality, experience and strengths

- The political background

- The property market

- The rules and regulations

- The people you meet

- The area where you live or operate

- The implementation, how you work

- The technology you make use of

- Your vision and your goals

Is it a Strategy or a Tool?

Before we move on, I would like to clarify the use of the term 'strategy' in this book. Some things can be a strategy to one person or a tool to another. Let's take an example:

Ben does some leafleting to find properties to buy at a discount, where his only aim is to buy property.

Craig does some leafleting to find properties that may be available to buy at a discount also, but in this case his aim is to find deals to sell on to other investors as he makes money from finders' fees.

In the above example, Ben is using sourcing as a **tool**, his focus being to buy property below market value for himself.

For Craig meanwhile, sourcing is his **strategy** – it is the focus of how he makes money in property; it IS his business.

The lines can be blurred: the two things can overlap. Ben may intend to do marketing only for his own purposes of buying, but if he gets more good leads than he can buy, or ones that are unsuitable, he could still make money by selling the deals on.

Craig, on the other hand, may intend only to sell deals on, but find an irresistible deal that he somehow then finds a way to buy... maybe through crowdfunding or a joint venture.

Any of the strategies in this book can be different things to different people and may be simply used as a tool or tactic for a particular situation.

In organising the chapters, there was always the risk of disappointing someone. For example, some have a main strategy that is actually niche, such as 'title splitting', but as this is a variation of development and is fairly self-explanatory, it did not get a chapter of its own. (*In case you're wondering, title splitting involves taking a big property, splitting it into flats and then putting them onto separate Titles so they can be sold individually at a higher price.*)

Strategies can be viewed from the perspective of someone providing the service or someone using it. Take letting agents for example: you might be one (it's your strategy) or use one (that's a tool); or do both, at different times in your career. But one thing is for sure, if you want to succeed on a big scale as a letting agent, you should definitely take notes from Glenn Ackroyd who founded the national lettings franchise EweMove with business partner David Laycock and later sold the company for a massive profit. (See Chapter 7 on Lettings and Appendix III for Glenn's questionnaire responses.)

Make That Change

Whether you need to change direction or choose to set off in a new direction, how best to make that change is a key question.

My favourite author, Brian Tracy, coined the phrase *zero based thinking*. He says:

> *"Think about all the activities you engage in today and ask yourself if there's anything you are doing today that, knowing what you now know, you wouldn't get into again if you could start over." He then goes on to say: "If there's anything you wouldn't get into today, then your next question should be 'how can I get out of this and how fast?'"*

His point about zero based thinking has helped me to see many things that I needed to let go of, such as some of my faraway properties that weren't working for me. It can be tempting to tell yourself that a particular bad experience won't happen again. Your pride is at stake, yet sometimes you need to admit it wasn't right for you and let it go, to stop it sapping your energy.

That's about negative changes, but what about positive ones? This book is not about encouraging you to try a lot of strategies, but rather to consider what's possible. You might choose one, or none, or add strategies one at a time to your main focus IF the time is right to try something new.

So how do you know if it's right? You don't, simply. The key thing is **how** you go about trying new things. It's about managing your resources, particularly your most precious resource – time, as well as capital; and making changes in a measured, cautious way.

The book *Strategic Planning Kit for Dummies* by Erica Olsen suggests that 90% of businesses are 'running without a plan', while emphasising the need to develop plans that are responsive to change when necessary:

"Strategy means consciously choosing to be clear about your company's direction in relation to what's happening in the dynamic environment. With this knowledge, you are much better positioned to respond proactively to the changing environment.

The term 'strategic planning' refers to a co-ordinated and systematic process for developing a plan for the overall direction of your endeavour for the purpose of optimising future potential.

The major assumption in strategic planning is that an organisation must be responsive to a dynamic, changing environment. The emphasis is on understanding how the environment is changing – and will change – and on developing organisational decisions that are responsive to these changes."

Trying anything new is a risk, so be sure to only take what risks you are willing to and/or can afford. When you have nothing or very little, risk is generally more palatable than when you have much to lose. Especially when you are young and hungry, you might 'risk it all' to set the world on fire – but when you are older and hopefully more established, the priority is not to crash and burn!

I would encourage older investors to engage with young entrepreneurs. They can bring an energy and freshness that can be both welcome and helpful. Young people don't have the same attachment to the past. Some older investors get caught up thinking about the way things were – what used to be possible, what things used to cost, which traps their thinking and keeps them stuck.

I was intrigued when I heard that fellow investor Kim Stones partnered up with young entrepreneur and rising star Ryan Carruthers. It's a good move. Aged 27, Ryan of Venture Property (www.venturepropertylincoln.co.uk) describes himself as *"very, very ambitious"*. See the questionnaire that Ryan completed for this book, in **Appendix III**.

To give you a taster, Ryan said: *"I use technology to manage every aspect of our business, which is a mixture of property development, HMO (professionals and students) and to find our deals for development. I have built a detailed tech system using slack and my team to pretty much automate the running of the portfolio which allows me to do what I do best, find deals!*

I have a VA (virtual assistant) in the Philippines, a bookkeeper – again, in the Philippines, and a self-employed cleaner / and viewer who does a lot of the move-ins and viewings."

Technology and apps can enhance your business. Ryan, as well as other young entrepreneurs, has helped me to become more aware of what has become widely known as prop-tech.

Prop-Tech

It has been said that while individuals may aim to improve by 10% a year, technology is improving at ten times that rate. If you're not using technology to enhance the performance of your business, you could be falling behind.

Prop-tech can help you to keep up. So, what exactly is prop-tech? The term is often used to refer to technology that can be useful in any part of the property industry to improve or refine services, products, methods and activity, from buying and renting to managing and maintaining residential and commercial property, including delivery and usage of services and utilities, purchases and sales.

Indeed, technology can be found in every area and aspect of property, just as it appears in all areas of life today – even the way we engage with each other. You can now do so much online, including arranging mortgages, dealing with solicitors, and researching properties to buy. Technology makes it easier and quicker to do most things, from banking to buying, from sourcing to selling.

Appendix I, which Ryan helped to inspire, lists a selection of some of the new era of technology and apps known as prop-tech that can help in your property business today.

What Do You Really, Really Want?

It is important to get clear not only about what strategies to adopt but also whether you even really want to invest in property, or do something else with your time and resources.

Do you want a passive investment or a business?

Property is best treated as a business, unless you can afford to pay others to fully manage everything for you.

You may be content with buying just one or two properties and that could be enough to give a good boost to your retirement income. Or you could choose to invest indirectly, for example in a crowdfunding project.

Time can be an issue. If you are still working full-time, you may choose to use a letting agent until you give up work when your property business grows sufficiently to sustain you, perhaps cutting costs by becoming a self-managing landlord.

As well as lifestyle, more choices include whether you are a spender or saver, how long term you plan (age and health may be factors), your financial goals, and your attitude to risk. Do you consider property riskier than savings or shares? Savings may be safe, but will not grow by much (if anything) and are likely to fall behind inflation in real terms over time. Property is more stable but less liquid than shares, which you could sell immediately and take the money within days, but shares are often riskier.

If you are a spender who lacks discipline around money, frankly you're unlikely to succeed in any business, particularly one of an investment nature such as property. It suits best those with self-discipline and a long-term perspective.

Some might have a lump sum but choose instead to have a home extension, or buy a home they can do up. Some people move every few years from one property to another: move to improve, getting bored once the work is done. I know a couple who have done very well this way and now live in a big house worth well over £1 million, with no rental properties to worry about, while continuing in their main careers which they enjoy.

You might want to buy a holiday home, in the UK or abroad. Of course, if you become successful in property, your goal can be to have the million-pound house, the holiday home and the lifestyle! (Holiday homes abroad are beyond the scope of this book however.)

Not everyone wants to do things in a 'big way' and we may not have the confidence at first to imagine big things for ourselves. It does not matter, though, whether you have confidence to start with or not – it's all about growth and we can all set goals and revise our vision as we make progress.

We grow through living and there is no better way to grow in confidence over time than in finding success by taking control of your destiny. You can start small if you wish. Dave and I started by taking lodgers in our twenties for ten years before we even started investing. We also tried various ideas, such as buying and selling second-hand furniture. It's ok to go at your own pace. But eventually you might conclude, as I did, that if you're going to think – you may as well think big!

The business of property can be set up any way you want, to suit your own personality, lifestyle and preferences; and is an excellent way to not only grow rich but to grow in every way. The variety of people I have met and interviewed for this book goes to show how varied our visions for ourselves and our lives can be… and it's all good.

So What Choices Will You Make?

Every choice and decision we make affects the look and feel of our lives. Some will favour certain attractions over others, such as whether to work from home or surround yourself with staff or co-workers. Every aspect of life is connected: your health, both physical and mental; family and relationships; environment; values.

Here are some further choices or distinctions that you might want to think about when considering whether the various strategies might suit you:

- High capital requirements vs low cost of entry;

- Active business vs a passive investment;

- Income vs capital gains;

- Low vs higher risk;

- Proven ideas vs new ideas;

- Good fit for you vs bad fit;

- Kitchen table vs having offices and staff;

- Long term vs short term.

For each strategy, I address the question of risk and what could go wrong; the potential downside, as well as what's good about it. Everything involves risk and you can't opt out by doing nothing as even doing nothing is a risk: the risk that you'll lose out on the gains you could have made had you done something!

When we do nothing, we learn nothing. When we do something, we learn and can adjust course.

We can adapt and survive.

The choices we make send us off in a certain direction and much of what we do on a daily basis rests on our habits. As the book *The Compound Effect* highlights, habits at first may not seem too impactful, but over the longer term will make a radical difference. You make your choices and then your choices make you. Every decision, no matter how slight, changes the trajectory of your life.

If you focus on one strategy until mastered, it becomes easier to do. Once that seems easy for you and you have systems and infrastructure in place, it could be time to add more strings to your bow if you want to. Always consider tax and finance in everything you do too.

So, let's now get started with looking at each strategy in turn.

Further Reading, Resources and References

The Power of Self-Discipline, Brian Tracy (Vanguard Press, 2011)

Strategic Planning Kit for Dummies, Erica Olsen, (John Wiley & Sons, 2nd edition 2012)

The Millionaire Next Door, Thomas J Stanley & W D Danko (Taylor Trade Publ, 2010)

The Compound Effect, Darren Hardy (Success Media Books, June 2010)

CHAPTER 2

SOURCING AND OPTIONS

*"The secret of getting ahead
is getting started."*

Mark Twain

Introduction

There are at least two great reasons for placing deal sourcing as the first strategy in this book:

1. There can be no great property investment or trade without first finding a great deal.

2. It can be a great place to start your property journey if you have very little money to begin.

Sourcing is the process of searching out great property deals, often through marketing, which sourcers either pass on to investors for a *finder's fee* or keep themselves. Investors may also engage in sourcing activity or use the services of others to source property for them. Either way, you need an appreciation of what's involved.

One of the high-profile experts most active in this area today is Sarah Poynton-Ryan, who hosts the Facebook group Property Sourcing Hub. Sarah hosts webinars, speaks at events and has educational YouTube videos on the subject, which are all very helpful. She also runs courses.

Another is Tina Walsh, who has written a book that is listed at the end of this chapter.

Whether your focus is on straightforward buy-to-let, rent-to-rent, HMOs, short-term lets, development, crowdfunding or any other strategy, deal sourcing should never be overlooked.

When a deal is found, it might be secured using an 'option agreement' which is a legal contract giving the buyer the right but not the obligation to buy.

It has to be said that people skills are crucial to becoming a successful sourcer. Some would say you need to be a good salesman or woman, but few people who are good with people like to think of it that way. They prefer to think in terms of empathising well with the client's needs and helping to solve their property problems. This is exactly what we were taught to do when I worked with A Quick Sale, as discussed in the next section.

Sourcing can be a way to make good money and is a great starting point for those starting out with little funds, but it takes more work, more determination and knowhow to find great deals than might at first seem to be the case.

Whether you are using the services of sourcers or finding deals for yourself, you need to be clear about what type of deal you are searching for, so you can focus your marketing efforts accordingly; and if a sourcer is to tailor their service to your requirements, they need to know!

Trust is an issue in this area and if you are using sourcers to find great deals, it is imperative that they are deserving of your trust. If you are being presented with deals, think of the quality and whether they are actually fully packaged deals or just leads with inadequate research.

Here is a summary of what's to come in this chapter:

- Buying below market value;

- Using option agreements to secure deals;

- How much you can earn as a sourcer;

- The process of sourcing: from lead generation to assessing the property and following up leads (speaking to clients); packaging up deals to sell to investors and getting paid.

Buying Below Market Value (BMV)

Buying below market value (BMV) is a great principle that has helped me and many others to get ahead quickly and can help you too. Buying BMV, meaning at a discount to the current open market value, is the core principle of all sourcing.

I joined a national franchise, from 2004-2009, called A Quick Sale, which trained and supported franchisees in marketing and securing property deals below market value. The motto of A Quick Sale's founder, Richard Watters, was: *"You make your money when you buy."*

By this he meant that if you can buy a property at say 30% below market value, you could immediately sell it on at market value and make money – hence your profit is assured. Whereas if you buy at market value, you can only make money by either adding value which will cost you time and money, or waiting for the market to rise.

So why would anyone sell their property at a price below the open market value? Basically, to achieve a quick sale. There can be a variety of reasons and predicaments that people find themselves in, as will be further considered later.

BMV is not without critics however, some even believing it's not very ethical. Others argue there is no such thing as *below market value* since someone is willing to sell you their property at the given price only because they were unable to sell it at a higher price, at least within the timescale they needed to do so. I find this a weak argument though. People sell below market value when they need a very quick sale. There could be said to be two values for a property – the retail market value and the quick sale value that an investor who can act fast is willing to pay. When you can offer clients a quick sale, you are giving them what they need when the open market cannot, creating a win: win situation.

Over the years some strategies have gone hand-in-hand very well with buying below market value such as *sale and rent back* where the seller would rent back the property after sale. This would normally be people on the brink of repossession who didn't want to lose their home but couldn't afford to keep up the mortgage repayments so were about to be evicted by their lender. By buying their house and allowing them to rent it back, the investor could provide a win: win situation. However, due to a minority of rogue traders the strategy was closed down by the government who regulated it to death. We were able to offer an alternative to one couple on the brink of repossession, however, by offering to buy their house and let them rent one of our other local properties instead.

Another strategy that worked for me with buying below market value was to buy property remote from where I live for **rent-to-buy** tenants (they rent while signing an option agreement to later buy the property). In these cases, I mostly handed over management of the property to EweMove.com to manage for me. Tenant buyers tend to treat properties as their own home, so the expenses are generally low. This has worked for me as below market value properties are easier to find in the north, and I don't like buying remotely unless I know I can put tenants in who will treat the place well and where I have a good agent in this specialist field.

The work and level of organisation involved in actively marketing for properties to buy below market value should not be underestimated and in fact became a full-time job for me during the years I was a franchisee of A Quick Sale.

Buying below market value needs to be looked at in conjunction with other factors, such as the property market cycle and location. If you are in an area where property prices are buoyant and rising, then putting all your energies into trying to find below market value deals could be a waste of time. Sometimes you might be better off being prepared to pay full price as you'll find very few people willing to sell below market value in such markets, and while you're wasting time on that, the market continues rising.

On the other hand, in a weak market or area where prices are not rising, it can be a lot easier to find deals below market value. In A Quick Sale, I found that I got far fewer deals in my southern area than some franchisees in other parts of the UK. Some of them got hundreds of leads a week and were doing several deals a month, whereas I got very few leads, leading to only four or five deals a year. I sometimes paid for deals from others in their areas.

If you are in an area where the market is hot and prices rising, where properties sell easily on the open market, you WILL get fewer leads than in areas where the market is cooler, stagnant or falling. In a cold area, you may get lots of people queuing up to sell you their properties 'below market value', but I know people who were buying a property a week in such areas before the crash of 2008 and later went bankrupt as prices fell to below what they paid, so be careful.

Options

Potential deals need to be secured and this is sometimes **but not always** achieved through the use of a type of contract with sellers called an **option**, so-called because it gives you the right – or option – to buy, but not the obligation, while it commits the vendor to sell to you, should you decide to go ahead with the purchase. Option agreements are often fair and necessary when sourcing, as it gives you time to line up an investor to buy, while preventing the seller from reneging on the deal or accepting another offer after already agreeing to yours.

Some vendors may be reluctant to sign an option agreement since it is likely to be unfamiliar, and even some solicitors may not be familiar with such contracts, so you may have to educate the client and encourage them to use a solicitor who understands such contracts.

You should also consult with and use a solicitor who is expert in setting up option contracts. A solicitor who is well known for this in property circles, who speaks at events – and is very entertaining – is Shimon Rudich of MS Law LLP Solicitors. (See contact details at the end of this chapter.)

However, there may be times when you decide to do the deal without bothering with an option agreement, for example if you have a trusted investor lined up who can act quickly, or perhaps if you are buying the property yourself. When I was in A Quick Sale and buying mostly for myself, I did not normally bother with option agreements. They are an added layer of complexity that is not always necessary, but can provide an extra safeguard and are more important in some situations than others.

A common scenario where options are useful is when a developer wishes to seek planning permission before committing to go ahead with the purchase of a property or piece of land. You can appreciate how the option is necessary when you consider that he may spend a lot of time and money on getting planning permission which will massively increase the value of the plot, at which stage it is essential that the deal does not fall through.

Options can be used in securing various deal types including assisted sales, buy-to-let, HMOs, rent-to-rent, short-term lets and development. If you intend passing on a deal, the contract with the vendor needs to be 'assignable', that is, transferable from the sourcer to his client, the buyer.

While options are often used primarily to secure deals for yourself or clients, their primary role may in some cases be to allow you to take over control of the property without purchasing it, for the option period.

There are broadly two main types of options:

- Purchase Options

- Lease Options

Purchase Options

A simple purchase option agreement is normally short-term and grants the holder the freedom to buy the property at an agreed price, within a specified period of time. This type of agreement is more straightforward than a lease option and is suitable for situations where you simply want to purchase or pass the deal on to an investor to purchase.

A purchase option is also used where a developer wants to secure the deal while seeking planning permission (as mentioned above). This is sometimes referred to as a 'planning gain' deal, where the chief aim is in the increased value once planning permission is gained.

Lease Options

A lease option is a purchase option with the added benefit for the holder to lease – or have use of – the property, during the option period.

This allows you, as the option holder, to take control of the property before purchase, so it can be let out, while making regular payments to the seller either directly or by paying the seller's mortgage direct.

Options have many key benefits compared to purchase, given the increasing number of adverse factors involved in the property-buying process, including:

- The high cost of stamp duty land tax (SDLT) when buying;

- The increasingly rigorous assessments required to secure mortgages, given the stringent PRA rules;

- The time it takes for lenders to process mortgage applications, which can take months;

- Big deposits required to buy;

- S24 affecting some investors' tax position badly, as mentioned in the Introduction.

When you use options, you can agree to buy the house at some future point in time, or to help the seller sell the house in a given time frame, while normally paying an agreed monthly sum to the vendor effectively to cover their mortgage payments and/or as rent.

You might take control of the property and rent it out for the duration of the option period and then, if you do not want to or cannot buy it yourself, you could sell the deal on to an investor (providing the terms of the agreement allowed: ie the option needs to be assignable).

You can then exercise your option to buy within the agreed term of the contract at a pre-agreed price and keep the difference between the price agreed and what you sell for.

Assisted Sales

As mentioned above, one scenario where options can be used is to secure your position when the deal is that you will help the vendor to sell their house in a given time frame. This is known as an assisted sale.

You might be wondering why the vendor would agree to this, versus just selling through an estate agent in the normal way. Well, it could be that the property has fallen into disrepair and that the owner has neither the cash nor the energy to refurbish the property so that it could sell for a decent price.

In this type of situation, you would normally agree a price with the vendor that they are happy with, while you take any net profit on the actual sale price above that figure. For example, say the vendor would accept £120,000 but the property is eventually sold for £150,000 – then you keep the net profit on the £30,000 uplift.

You might additionally agree to a profit share over a certain level. Say the property sells for £170,000. If it was in your contract with the vendor that you share profits 50/50 on anything over £150,000, then you would split the extra £20,000 to get half each.

This strategy saves the investor a whole raft of big expenses that he would have if he bought the property, such as the conveyancing costs of buying and selling, mortgage costs and the time taken to apply for mortgages (plus, it is getting harder for some investors to even qualify for mortgages); as well as not having to pay stamp duty – a big bonus! Of course, whilst exciting, there must be a willing seller for this type of deal to come about.

I met Sunny Kapur at a networking event who does just that: he is a London-based investor, specialising in assisted sales as his main strategy. Sunny explained that it works very well for him as he doesn't have to buy the properties and it appeals to his sense of fairness too, helping vendors to sell by undertaking refurbishments for them (with an option in place) instead of buying their property BMV.

How Much Can You Earn as a Sourcer?

Let's say that your target income is £5,000 per month. That's £60,000 per year. Finder's fees vary depending on a variety of factors, but are typically between £1,000 - £5,000 per deal, so you could make that much if you can find between 1-5 deals per month to package up and sell. Of course, you will have expenses such as the cost of advertising, but you can keep costs low if you need to in the early days.

Work backwards from your goal for annual income as a sourcer:

£60,000 income per annum for example =

£5,000 per month =

2 deals per month

At average fee to buyer of deal of £2,500

You can get started part time while doing other things too, even a day job if you're just getting started. You can structure your business so that you don't have to visit the properties yourself. You should always make initial contact by phone with vendors, then later you can either visit yourself, outsource the matter, or require your investor to visit the property. This means that you're not restricted geographically to sourcing deals (although you should always have local knowledge or access to a trusted person who does).

People often pass deals on because they are not in a position to buy property themselves, or they pass on some if they can't buy as many as they find. Sarah Poynton-Ryan who teaches deal sourcing (as mentioned earlier) explains that she mainly finds deals for rent-to-rent for herself and passes on any others. She rents property from landlords on a single-let and, with their permission, rents the property out as a multi-let which generates a higher income – keeping the difference, generating a net profit of around £1,000 per property per month.

Rules and Regulations to be aware of

Those presenting deals to others are legally deemed to be acting as estate agents and are subject to the same regulations accordingly. Tina Walsh, a former police officer, has written a book on the matter: *Property Sourcing Compliance*.

Estate agency type work is defined as *"Introducing or brokering a deal between a seller and a buyer as a business"* and property sourcers fall into this category. As such they must have professional indemnity insurance, register with a property redress scheme (see the references section at the end of this chapter), and register for data protection supervision and with HMRC for money laundering supervision.

The Seven Stages of Deal Sourcing

This section takes a closer look at the various stages of deal sourcing and the processes involved at every stage. If you want to do deal sourcing, you need to be aware that it generally involves a lot of work and a complex set of tasks which need to be kept track of at every stage.

Here is a summary of the seven stages that will be considered in this section:

1. Lead generation

    a. Who is likely to sell below market value?

    b. Marketing and advertising

2. Managing your workload

    a. Outsourcing some of the work

    b. Should you use a CRM system?

    c. Following up on leads

3. Determining the valuation

    a. Rightmove and Zoopla

    b. Due diligence all round

4. Dealing with enquiries from vendors

    a. Using a telephone questionnaire

    b. Negotiating the terms of the deal

5. Packaging up deals to sell on

6. Building a database of investors

7. Presenting deals to investors and getting paid

Lead Generation

In order to generate leads, or enquiries, you will need to do some marketing and advertising. Firstly, think who your target audience or market are? Then, where they may be looking; and, what type of material or websites do they read or take notice of?

Who is likely to sell below market value?

There can be various reasons why people need a quick sale. It is sometimes suggested you consider "the 3D's":

- Debt, including being on the brink of repossession

- Divorce, or other relationship estrangement

- Death, including probate situations and inherited property

Unpleasant though it may sound, there is some truth in that, and it's worth remembering that while making money may be your top priority at the time, it is not necessarily so for people whose lives have been turned upside down by such unfortunate events. The fact is, they have a problem, and it is your role to offer a solution that gets them out of a fix and that is acceptable to them.

Further reasons for wanting a quick sale may include:

- Property won't sell due to poor state (ideal for assisted sales, mentioned above)

- Emigration: when emigrating, the seller may have little time to sort out their affairs

- Downsizers: including people who need to move to more suitable property in a hurry for health reasons

- Upsizers. I met Sachin Vekaria of CrowdWithUs (see Chapter 10: Crowdfunding) at a London networking event who said he finds people whose fortunes have improved to the extent they can't wait to move!

Marketing and advertising

What budget you allocate for marketing will partly depend on the returns you get and how fruitful the campaign is.

I spoke to fellow investor Charlie Burnett who said he was spending up to £40,000 a month marketing for below-market value deals including television advertising at one time which was working for him. Most of us start on a more modest budget!

He now uses Facebook for advertising his restaurant (Max & Ben's Bistro, in Auchterarder in Scotland) on the basis of 'pay per click': you choose an area, say how much you're willing to spend and for how long, then pay each time someone clicks on your advert. I asked if he thought it would work for property sourcing and he said yes, it would.

Bear in mind that marketing can produce unfocused results unless it's highly selective and you could attract enquiries from properties you don't especially want, although any property should be wanted by someone at the right price, so have a database of investors that you can pass deals on to.

The most focused form of marketing has got to be leafleting, as you can target postcodes down to exact levels or even particular properties. However, it is also one of the most expensive and time-consuming. It's best to try various things and see what works for you.

Think of the cost of marketing as an investment, remembering that one deal could return a profit of £50,000 or more in due course. I have sold properties that I bought during my time in A Quick Sale Ltd for £100,000 and more than I paid a few years ago!

While your requirements may be limited, if you have investors that you could pass deals on to, then you can make money as a sourcer. Here is a list of some forms of advertising that sourcers use:

- Leafleting (have a targeted message with a clear call to action "Call Now!")

- Local papers (national for very high budgets only); classified ads can be effective as well as cheaper than display or box ads

- Look out for private property sales via Gumtree and in papers

- Try contacting landlords advertising properties to rent – you may find some tired landlords who could be happy with a rent-to-rent deal or even to sell

- Facebook advertising (as mentioned above)

- Make sure local estate and letting agents know what your requirements are, as they could bring deals your way. It's important to build such relationships upon trust and by showing that you are an action taker

- Look around your neighbourhood for distressed-looking properties where there might be a problem you can help to solve, and try contacting the owners

- Let solicitors know what sort of deals you are looking out for as they may have clients who need help

- Attend networking meetings, including non-property related ones such as BNI (Business Network International), and tell people what you do

- You could try auctions, although beware since properties are not necessarily cheaper at auction. Some people make a niche of offering low on unsold lots after auction; while others sell at auction successfully.

The form of advertising, or otherwise searching for leads, that is most effective for you will at least partly depend on your requirements – on what you are looking for. What works for seeking residential properties to buy BMV to let, will be very different from what works if you are looking for rent-to-rent deals for example, and different again for potential development sites. *(The main assumption here is towards targeting residential sales, as searching for rent-to-rent and development deals are dealt with in the chapters on each of those strategies.)*

People often need to see your advert or leaflet several times before they will believe you're not a *fly by night*, here today and gone tomorrow. It's best if you can repeat adverts or leafleting several times, even as much as every week for several weeks, so you should budget for this.

Managing Your Workload

The key thing is to test and measure everything, to see if it's working. Bear in mind that if you are paying to do marketing for leads, then each one has a cost and should be treated as valuable.

You also need to be incredibly organised and follow up leads, especially if you get a lot of them.

Outsourcing some of the work

Sourcing can become a full-time occupation if you want it to be. Of course, that will depend on whether you enjoy the work and if it proves worthwhile. Remember, you can start small and be in control of how much of your time you allow it to take up.

You could outsource parts of the work that you don't like, or that are time-consuming and of little monetary value, such as leaflet distribution or taking initial phone calls. Some people employ assistants or VAs (virtual assistants), which you can find online at reasonable rates.

Should you use a CRM system?

A central customer relationship management system (or CRM), helps to keep track of leads and ensure regular follow-up. We used a CRM when I was in A Quick Sale, which was offered as part of the franchise system.

If you are starting independently in a small way, you could use a simple Excel spreadsheet and calendar reminders or other software. Podio.com is mentioned in Appendix I, which includes a CRM.

People often need several follow-ups before they may be ready to commit to selling to you. They may want time to think it over, talk to family, or see if they can find another solution. A CRM can help to remind you to make follow-up calls and to keep track of what has been discussed with each client so far. When you have quite a few leads, it can be surprisingly difficult to recall the details of each one just in your head!

Following up on leads

Given that leads cost you time and money to get in the first place, it is imperative that you do not waste them. Make sure to follow up again – and again!

Whether you use a CRM or not, it is always worth staying in touch as long as the client agrees. You never know when they might be ready to act – and you don't want to lose the deal to a competitor just because you forgot to follow-up. We used to call leads on a weekly basis in A Quick Sale.

Whatever system or software you use, make careful notes about any discussions you have had with potential vendors, as you will forget when you have a lot of them to manage. Include dates of all communications and any offers you may have made, even if they were not immediately accepted. Many vendors will be fine with you keeping in touch, so make sure you set yourself reminders in your calendar or CRM system to do so as often as necessary.

Some people are naturally hesitant but may say yes later, when they've got to know you through regular contact and have built more trust.

It can take seven or more times of making contact before some enquirers feel comfortable enough to consider selling their property to you. It's a similar principle with advertising and leafleting: marketing should not be done just once.

Determining the Valuation

When you get leads, eventually you will have to value the property, assessing the open market value (OMV) and rental yield, as well as any cost of works, to ascertain the purchase price that will give you the required return on investment (ROI).

Property valuation is said to be more of an art than a science. Nevertheless, you need to be as accurate as possible in your estimation of the value now and the potential value after refurbishment, in order to secure a good deal.

If a property is standard and of a type that has plenty of like or comparable properties nearby – preferably including ones that have sold fairly recently – then it should be straightforward to gauge the value. However, there are various potential issues that you need to be wary of, even then.

If on the other hand the property is in any way unusual or unique, including commercial buildings, land plots and many potential developments, then it is likely to be best to get professional help from a qualified surveyor to value the property.

Assuming you are dealing with a standard type of property, in the first instance you should check comparable prices (sometimes called 'comps'). This can often be done fairly simply by looking on Rightmove and Zoopla for similar properties nearby and what they have sold for. You can also do this at the Land Registry.

Rightmove and Zoopla

My first port of call is normally www.rightmove.co.uk. If you click on the "House Prices" tab at the top of the page on Rightmove, it brings down a set of choices including the following:

- **Sold house prices**: Provides a list in order of most recent first, of properties sold in the same postcode. You can vary the list by choosing property type, search within a quarter of a mile, and so on.

- **Price comparison report**: In addition to showing recently sold properties in the target area, this report includes properties that are currently on the market as well as ones removed from the market and properties available to rent. Again, you can vary the criteria. Strangely, when I tried an example search, I found the default setting 'within a quarter of a mile' did not include properties in the actual postcode! You do have to be careful when using these searches.

- **Market trends**: This is a good feature, showing how prices have changed in the area. Again, you can change the variables for the property type being considered, or number of years.

- **Property valuation**: Only do this if you want to invite estate agents to value your property!

On the 'buy' tab at Rightmove you can find an 'investors' page, where you can sign up for a free newsletter for the area you are interested in which will give you similar information by regular email newsletters. You can set this up for as many postcodes as you wish.

You can also set up email alerts for property types and locations of interest. For example, I set one up for three-bed houses in the area where we own many, in order to keep an eye on current prices.

Zoopla offers similar facilities, which you can also find and explore from tabs at the top of the site; it also has articles about wider property investment ideas such as investing in REITs (Real Estate Investment Trusts) as part of your pension arrangements.

One of the things that many investors like about www.zoopla.co.uk is that under the advanced search function (of properties for sale) you can include keywords – so you could look for example for properties that are listed as "in need of refurbishment" or other such terms.

Due diligence all round

In addition to using Rightmove and Zoopla, you may need to involve a surveyor in more unusual cases to help with the valuation. Alternatively, you could ask a friendly estate agent to help.

A word of caution from my own experience about valuing property: I once bought a house after the vendor responded to my direct marketing which was in a lovely road of big properties. The first problem was that the properties varied in size and style, but what I also overlooked at the time was that the garden of this particular property backed onto a motorway much more closely than most of the others in the street which of course down-valued it, or should have.

I drove by, but that's all, as the owners were living abroad and the property was empty. I even asked a local estate agent to drive by and they didn't notice this either. It was only when you got out of the car that you could tell the extent of the problem – particularly standing in the back garden.

I ended up over-paying and had to let it out for a few years, waiting for values to rise; but I did eventually sell it for a profit!

It is not only the property that you need to do due diligence on, but also the people you engage with. As a sourcer, you need to assess both your sellers and buyers. Get ID and contact details. Use contracts such as lease options where appropriate.

With buyers (/investors) you might want to use a 'non-disclosure agreement' (NDA), sometimes called a 'confidentiality agreement', which is designed to prevent them from using the information about a potential deal, other than for the intended purpose of seeing whether they are interested in buying the property through you and paying your finder's fees.

Sourcers' views vary on the use of NDAs. Some feel they are not worth using as they could be difficult to enforce but others see them as worthwhile, not least as a matter of principle to ensure the investor understands that it is a serious matter for the sourcer to share such information. Of course, trust is an issue whether using an NDA or not and it is always preferable to work with trustworthy individuals.

If you are looking to joint venture (JV) to buy property, it is especially important to know your JV partner's financial background, as your finances could be badly affected as well as your credit rating by that association. It would be reasonable to request references from their accountant and/or solicitor.

You can look people up at Companies House to see what companies they own or are involved with. You can also Google people's names (some suggest followed by the word 'scam') to see if anything bad is revealed about them.

Establishing the difference between the value of a property in its current state and the potential value after refurb or development involves making a good estimation of costs for the work required. This obviously depends on the amount and nature of the work, and can vary from fairly straightforward to estimate (for example, the cost of a new kitchen is not that difficult to ascertain) to much more complex in the case of development, when it could even be necessary to involve a quantity surveyor.

Of course, you also need to convince the vendor that their property may not be worth as much as the one down the road that recently sold in tip-top condition!

Bear in mind when considering a purchase, that any project you undertake will use time and financial resources and therefore has an opportunity cost which should also be taken into account. This is particularly pertinent when you are presented with various possibilities.

Dealing with Enquiries from Vendors

When dealing with vendors, be prepared to ask questions about the property as well as their situation. Initial conversations are often by phone, so have a telephone questionnaire readily to hand. Appendix II includes a telephone questionnaire you may use to guide the conversation, as further discussed below.

Using a telephone questionnaire

You might wish to vary the questionnaire to suit the exact steps in your procedures. When I was in A Quick Sale, initial calls were handled by a central call centre (you could use a virtual assistant (VA) or personal assistant (PA) service, which you can find online). The call centre would take basic information from the client such as their contact details and the property type, so by the time of my first call to the client I would already have done some initial research, looking at comparables and seeing whether their property could be found for sale online.

Summary of Telephone Questionnaire *(Full details in Appendix II):*

- Client contact details

- What marketing is being responded to

- Type of property

- Their estimation of value

- Reason for sale

- Their circumstances and story

- Property information: type, number of beds, receptions, conservatory, extensions, etc

- When built and construction

- What state or condition is the property in?

- Environment, neighbourhood

- Who lives there? Who's on the title? Do they agree to the sale?

- Mortgage: lender, mortgage amount; any other loans secured or unsecured?

- Leasehold info if applicable: lease/services, etc

- Market value? Where do they get the idea from? Is it listed with an estate agent? Where?

- What I'll do next…

You may wish to add further questions especially for particular types of deal, such as for rent-to-rent where you might ask what timescales the landlord is looking to lease the property for; or development, where for example you may want to ask about any planning history.

Negotiating the terms of the deal

Investors who are willing to pay finder's fees to sourcers would normally expect to buy property at a greater discount than they could get by just going to an estate agent and haggling on price themselves. As a ballpark figure, most would expect at least a 10% discount to the open market value, or more – even as much as 20%, depending on location.

The first thing that you and your investors need to be realistic about is location. I have found prices are generally a lot less elastic in locations where demand is high and exceeds the supply of properties to market. In areas where the market is hot, it can be a lot harder to find bargains. Indeed, in some markets properties may go over the market value, even having to go to 'sealed bids'. Sourcing in such markets can be hard and the number of opportunities limited, but on the upside, if you get a potential deal, it can be very valuable!

At some stage, either you or your investor should be willing to visit the property. Personally, I always used to visit the property myself after the initial call with the client as I felt it was important to make a full assessment of the property and to build rapport with the client too. I was interested to learn that Sarah Poynton-Ryan says that she doesn't normally visit properties but asks her potential investors to do so. I was mostly buying for myself whereas Sarah has made a big business out of sourcing and cast a wide net, so it warrants a very different approach.

When presenting your offer to the vendor, you should be prepared to show comparables and to reason with them about why you think their property might be worth less than they may have hoped. This needs to be dealt with sensitively as people can get upset with your suggestion of what you would be willing to pay. It is best to prime them beforehand, by making sure they understand that they have chosen to engage with a 'quick sale' company and remind them of why they stated that they need an urgently quick sale.

It could be good to have a well-presented report to show the vendor, so they see the comparables and all your estimates of costs for any necessary works, if applicable, to bring the property up to scratch – such as the cost of a new boiler, or a new kitchen.

You must be ready and able to act very quickly. Have speedy solicitors lined up, finance readily available and, if passing the deal to an investor, make sure they can act fast too.

If you were hoping for a 15% discount but the vendor is only willing to offer 10%, it would be good if you have a choice of investors that the deal might be suitable for, or even a good estate agent who may be willing to work with you to find an investor for the deal.

Building a Database of Investors

Unless you intend to buy all the deals you source yourself, you will need to have some investors to pass deals onto. You should aim for the number of investors to match your sourcing efforts, so if you may have the occasional deal in a particular location only, then you may only need one or two investors who could be interested. Some sourcers aim to find properties to the requirements of individual investors, and that can work too.

But if you are advertising widely on a bigger scale and getting plenty of leads, then you will need a larger database of investors to match.

Presenting Deals to Investors and Getting Paid

When presenting deals to investors, you might first tell just one or two individuals who you think may be interested according to the deal criteria they are after. You might tell them the property type, possibly send a photo (but not the whole address) with the open market value (OMV) and the purchase price and rental value. You might follow this up with an email, or send an email newsletter with details of deals available to your list, giving brief details such as the example below (not a real address!):

When you are sourcing for others on a big scale, you will most likely have investors on your list that you do not know well if at all. Sadly, not everyone we come across is trustworthy and it can be difficult to know who those people are until after they let you down.

Having said that, the trust issue certainly works both ways. I have used the services of several sourcers over the years and had some great deals, but not all were equally good. I found the quality varied and there were times when I was quite naïve, let's say.

The facts

Bedrooms: 2
Type: Semi-detached
Tenure: Freehold
Construction: Standard
Ex-council: No
Year Built: 1982

Features

Heating: Gas central
Parking: Off-road
Double glazing: Yes
Gardens: back & front
Garage: No
Extensions: No
Other: Kitchen was new 2 years ago; new boiler.

Price Comparables:

22/10/2107: 41 Cranford Road
Semi, sold £120,000
09/04/2017: 4 Cranford Road,
Semi, sold £123,000

Cranford Road, Oldham, OL1

OMV	£120,000
Net Price	£96,000
Discount	20%
Estimated Rent	£480 pcm
Yield	6%

Nevertheless, sourcers find that a minority of people will ask for details of deals but then try to wriggle out of paying for them. It is important to manage the process in such a way as to minimise the risk of that happening.

One way in which you can do this is by not sending out the full address details initially. People may enquire from brief initial details on your website or the list that you send out. You should always get them to provide contact details in the first place, such as name, email and phone number. Some sourcers, as mentioned earlier, get investors to sign a non-disclosure agreement.

If an investor is interested after some but not all details are sent, you might ask them for a reservation fee, say £995, before you send full details including the address. This will help to weed out time wasters and rogues.

I believe most people are good though, and as long as you take all sensible measures to protect the valuable information about the deals you have worked hard to find, then you could make a very good living as a property sourcer. This strategy lends itself well to being done in conjunction with other strategies, such as rent-to-rent – which is the subject of the next chapter.

Further Reading, Resources and References

Sarah Poynton-Ryan hosts the FB group: "Property Sourcing Hub" at: https://www.facebook.com/groups/285111485269879/ There is a lot of detail, discussion, good advice and best practice discussed there. Sarah also hosts webinars, speaks at events and runs courses in Sourcing – in addition to running her own successful sourcing company.

Shimon Rudich, Partner at MS Law LLP Solicitors. Email: shimonrudich@ms-law.co.uk.

Investor mentioned in Assisted Sales section: Sunny Kapur, email: sunnyrkapur@gmail.com

Tina Walsh, a former police officer, has written a book: *Property Sourcing Compliance: Keeping You on The Right Side of the Law*, Tina Walsh (Sept 2017)

For details of property redress schemes: https://www.gov.uk/redress-scheme-estate-agencies

How does this strategy appeal to you?

Rate this strategy, on a scale from 0 – 10, for the following factors:

0 . 1 . 2 . 3 . 4 . 5 . 6 . 7 . 8 . 9 . 10   **Time**

0 . 1 . 2 . 3 . 4 . 5 . 6 . 7 . 8 . 9 . 10   **Money**

0 . 1 . 2 . 3 . 4 . 5 . 6 . 7 . 8 . 9 . 10   **Risk**

0 . 1 . 2 . 3 . 4 . 5 . 6 . 7 . 8 . 9 . 10   **Appeal**

0 . 1 . 2 . 3 . 4 . 5 . 6 . 7 . 8 . 9 . 10   **Knowledge**

0 . 1 . 2 . 3 . 4 . 5 . 6 . 7 . 8 . 9 . 10   **Aptitude**

0 . 1 . 2 . 3 . 4 . 5 . 6 . 7 . 8 . 9 . 10   **Tax**

CHAPTER 3

RENT-TO-RENT

"Dream Big; Start Small; Act Now!"

Robin Sharma

Rent-to-rent is a hot topic in property today, particularly as it can be started with very little capital or start-up costs. It can go hand-in-hand with sourcing too: almost as a natural extension, keeping deals which are available for rent-to-rent, while passing on others where the owner wants to sell.

Many of the strategies discussed in this book have become fashionable in response to difficulties investors face – perhaps none more so than rent-to-rent. Many have turned to these strategies because simple buy-to-let purchases may be out of reach for a variety of reasons, including the size of deposit required, difficulty in obtaining mortgage finance and tax issues.

The term *rent-to-rent* is relatively new and the idea has gained in popularity, but the basic concept has been around for much longer, as we shall see.

The strategy attracts some criticism, as there is a lot that can go wrong or be done wrong. But there is a right way to legitimately go about rent-to-rent. If you are keen to find out how to go about things the right way and what to watch out for on the downside, then read on…

What is Rent-to-Rent?

The basic premise of rent-to-rent is that you pay the property owner a set amount each month and then rent the property often on a room-by-room basis as a multi-let or house in multiple occupation (HMO) for higher returns, keeping the difference.

The diagrams below illustrate an example of a house where the landlord was getting £1,000 per month renting as a single let on a house with 3 bedrooms, a separate living room, dining room and kitchen. The rent-to-renter then rents the property as an HMO with four lettable rooms, at £500 per month for each room, using the separate living room as an additional bedroom:

| House as Single Let | Bed 1 | Bed 2 | Bed 3 | Rent £500 | Rent £500 | Rent £500 |
| Rent = £1,000 per month | Living room | Dining room | Kitchen | Rent £500 | Dining room | Kitchen |

This example produces total returns of £2,000 per month, while the dining room could possibly be used too, giving five lettable rooms generating £2,500 per month.

The landlord might be happy to receive £1,000 per month, maybe even less if you can guarantee the rent. You will have some expenses, as you would normally take responsibility for the utility bills and council tax, which could be say £350 per month, but then you keep the rest. So your net profit per property could be between £650 and £1,150 per month.

Some operators also use rent-to-rent for serviced accommodation, aiming for even higher returns. Elements of various other strategies can be used in rent-to-rent, and I highly recommend you learn more by reading the relevant chapters such as Buy-to-Let (Chapter 4), HMOs (Chapter 5) and Serviced Accommodation (Chapter 6).

The advantages of rent-to-rent for operators:

Rent-to-rent can have many advantages and attractions, including:

- Properties can be controlled without the costs involved in buying;

- No need for large sums of money for deposits as when buying;

- Can be done even if circumstances make it difficult to get a mortgage;

- Avoid the risk that property could go down in value;

- Avoid the risk of interest rate rises;

- Avoid adverse taxation that might apply if you had mortgages;

- It's quick to set up. You could view a property with the owner and take it on within days, then rent it out in within a week if no works are required;

- It gives you immediate positive cashflow, so it can be a fast route to financial freedom.

When you do rent-to-rent, it is important that you set up contracts in the right way so that you do not fall foul of any regulations. We will look at various set ups that exist but you should seek legal advice and get help drawing up contracts. However, before we go further, let's answer the first question that many people ask:

Why Would a Property Owner Agree to Rent-to-Rent?

There can be many reasons why a property owner (the landlord) might agree to such an arrangement, including:

- Guaranteed rent or other monthly payments. Perhaps the biggest attraction for landlords – to know they will receive a reliable, fixed sum each month come what may;

- Length of the agreement: Rent-to-rent agreements are often for 3-5 years and this can suit owners who want to own their asset for the long term without having to give it more frequent thought. The longer the agreement, the greater the peace of mind, for some;

- Passive income: the landlord may put a high value on the fact it allows for more passive income, without the usual landlord concerns;

- The owner may have experienced hassles renting out their property in the past, which they are keen to avoid in future;

- They may be tired either physically or mentally of the strain of being a landlord;

- The house may be in a poor state, which they may not have the funds or wherewithal to sort out.

If you are a landlord, it's important to consider all your options carefully. We all have times as landlords when we feel thoroughly disheartened, maybe a bad tenant has trashed your property, or you're just tired of the grind. But there is a huge level of trust required in handing over control of your properties and I would be most keen to know I was dealing with a top-notch person or organisation.

As a rent-to-rent operator, you absolutely must let the owner know your intentions when you take a property on, not least because the landlord needs to ensure the property is covered by suitable insurance and that they are not in breach of their mortgage when the property is let as an HMO. Some properties may have covenants stating they must only be occupied by single family units and must not be sub-let, particularly so with flats.

We will look further at the risks and consider what can go wrong later in this chapter, from the point of view of both landlords and rent-to-rent operators. But first...

How Much Money Can You Make?

As a low-cost start strategy, rent-to-rent tends to attract those starting with very little money, but be aware that there will be some expenses: you will most likely need up to a few thousand pounds to set up each property initially, so if you have no money whatsoever, you might want to partner up with someone who does in order to get started.

Earlier we looked at an example of how the model works. Here's a reminder of the cashflow that is possible from a typical rent-to-rent set up with five lettable rooms, each rented for £500 per month. In this example, monthly expenses are £500 per month:

Rent received: £500 x 5 (per person, per month) = **£2,500 pcm**

Utilities, council tax and other costs such as cleaners = **£500 pcm**

Rent to landlord = **£1,000 pcm**

Your net monthly profit = **£1,000 pcm**

With five such houses, your income could be £60,000 per year. Depending on rents in your area and the number of rooms, you might calculate your profit to be £500 per month per property. Don't forget to take into account that:

- The costs may be greater;

- There may be voids you need to factor in;

- The properties may only have four rooms, not five;

- The rent per room may be less;

- Or the rent to the landlord more.

Research your area. What properties are you targeting? What are the rents in your area? What deal can you negotiate with the landlord?

If you only make £500 per month per property but have six by the end of one year, that's still an income of £36,000. Many people would be happy with that for a startup business.

Scaling Up Your Rent-to-Rent Business

If you are starting with very little money, you will need to grow your business organically. If you are starting with more money, either your own or other people's, you can grow your business more quickly.

Around £3,000 is probably the minimum you should start with as you need to allow some cash for refurbishment as well as possible adaptations (including the fitting of fire doors if you are turning a single-let property into an HMO). Here's an example of how your rent-to-rent business could grow from this starting point. (This is a simplified example for the purposes of illustration; in practice you would allow extra time for setting up each property):

- House 1: Refurb and other costs to set up £3,000;

- Net monthly profit after the first month = £1,000;

- Net monthly profit after three months = £3,000 (breakeven point, as that's what you invested initially);

- Then in month 4, you can use the £3,000 profit generated to take on house number 2;

- From month 4, profit now £2,000 per month so it takes only two months before you can take on house number 3;

- With three houses, you are generating £3,000 per month so can take on house number 4 after just one more month;

- Notice that the rate of growth escalates as you take on more properties, so your rate of growth speeds up the more properties you take on.

If you start with a larger sum initially, say £12,000, you can get 4 houses from the outset and the business can grow exponentially at a much faster rate.

I hope this illustrates how the business can mushroom in growth even from a modest start.

Initial Costs to Set Up the Property

When you acquire a property, there are bound to be some initial set-up costs. It is often the case that you take a property which has been rented out as a single let previously, with the aim of turning it into an HMO. You may need to:

- Fit fire doors;

- Provide furniture;

- Undertake a general refurbishment.

Remember that it is not your property and your contract will be for a limited time, usually 3-5 years. It is recommended that you spend no more than 4-6 months' equivalent of net profits at the most.

Don't assume you should pay for everything. Your agreement with the landlord should specify their responsibilities. Landlords will normally continue to be responsible for matters relating to the building such as things covered by their general buildings insurance – the 'externals' including the roof, risk of subsidence and so on; as well as the gutters, soffits and fascias. They should also assume responsibility for boilers and the heating system, as well as fire safety and the electrical system. All this should be in your contract.

Setting Up a Rent-to-Rent Agreement

There are various forms of rent-to-rent agreement that could be used, depending on the circumstances, but the only ones you should normally consider are:

1. **Guaranteed Rent - Management Agreement:** This is the type of agreement that it **IS** recommended you use where the property owner has a mortgage as it is effectively no different from a letting agent's *guaranteed rent* agreement.

2. **Lease Option Agreement:** If there is a mortgage lender, you should check if this type of agreement would be allowed; otherwise, a lease agreement could offer the best type of contract as the clauses and terms can be very flexible as agreed with the owner.

3. A simple **Assured Shorthold Tenancy Agreement (AST)** is NOT normally advisable, as your rent-to-rent arrangements would amount to sub-letting and could invalidate the owner's insurance or mortgage compliance – although it could be used where there's no mortgage and where the insurance allows. Most leases on flats do not allow sub-letting either, so an AST is very likely to be unsuitable for flats, even where there is no mortgage.

You should never take a property on a single assured shorthold tenancy agreement (AST) and then go and let it out as an HMO without permission, as that could put the landlord's insurance and mortgage terms and conditions at risk of being in breach and land you in a lot of trouble.

It is usually best to use a management agreement between yourself and the landlord, so that you are positioned as the landlord's agent. *(Note also the overlap in this strategy with letting agents, further discussed in Chapter 7.)* Or alternatively, use a lease option type of agreement.

These types of agreement have in fact been used for many years, for example:

- Letting agents such as Northwood offer guaranteed rent;

- Housing Associations and others lease landlords' properties;

- Lease options can be used effectively for rent-to-rent.

The exact contract and agreements will depend on the circumstances of all parties involved.

Using a Management Agreement

A management agreement is probably the most straightforward type of rent-to-rent agreement you can use in terms of being compliant with the property owner's mortgage, insurance and other conditions.

Bear in mind that you are effectively acting as a letting agent by offering this type of agreement. While letting agents are not currently required to have professional qualifications there are strong calls for this to be changed, so you may in future have to get qualified and even join a professional body and ombudsman scheme too.

The well-known franchise lettings and estate agents, Northwood, are a prime example of an agent that has been offering a management agreement that is in effect like rent-to-rent to landlords for over 20 years, with the bonus of **guaranteed rents**. They make their money by offering below market rents to landlords and do not rent the properties out as HMOs but simply charge higher rents than the landlord receives, the difference being higher than the usual letting agent fees for the privilege of guaranteed rents.

Note that all their offices belong to a Property Ombudsman scheme and Northwood was a founding member of SAFEagent campaign set up by the National Approved Letting Scheme (NALS).

Using a Lease Option Agreement

Lease agreements give you the greatest flexibility in drawing up a contract with the landlord, but if there is a mortgage, the lender may not agree to such a contract, so you need to check. Always seek advice from a solicitor in respect of any form of legal contracts, preferably one experienced in this field.

Before you even ask a solicitor, it is worth educating yourself as thoroughly as possible and seeking advice from other experienced operators, to help you to initially consider every point that you would want included in your legal agreement with the property owner, before getting a solicitor to draft the agreement based on such 'heads of terms' as you agree with the property owner.

Heads of terms is a phrase used to describe the outline of the terms of your agreement and understanding with the property owner, which sets out the terms agreed in principle in the course of your negotiations, pending the formal drafting up of the legal agreement by solicitors.

The heads of terms should include such things as:

- The length or 'term' of the agreement;

- The amount of any deposit to be paid;

- The amount of rent charged and any rent reviews to be included;

- What insurances are to be in place and who is responsible for each;

- Outgoings such as utilities and council tax – who pays;

- Maintenance issues: who is responsible for what repairs and maintenance;

- Whether there is to be a 'break clause' (which gives you the flexibility to get out of the agreement early if necessary);

- The condition the property should be returned in and what is fair wear and tear;

- Ground rent and service charge liability in the case of leasehold properties;

- Who will take responsibility for making sure mortgage payments are made.

Mortgages

Meeting the terms of the mortgage is ultimately the property owner's responsibility, but you should help them to understand what they need to know about compliance. You should ideally look at the mortgage contract with them and recommend they make sure any agreement you would come to will not violate the terms of the mortgage.

The owner should in particular check their mortgage to see whether HMOs are allowed, if this is the intention under your agreement.

Note that if you need an HMO licence, you will need to make sure the mortgage will allow it because as part of the HMO licence application, many councils will contact the mortgage lender.

How do you make sure the landlord makes his mortgage payments? It comes down to trust. If there comes a time they cannot make their payments, you could offer to buy the property below market value if you are able to, or consider selling it on to another investor for a fee, if acceptable to the owner.

Insurance

It is important for all parties that the correct insurances are in place. Consult with an insurance expert regarding which insurances are needed.

The property owner should have buildings insurance in place, but you could become a named party on it. You should have a clause in your contract to specify what type of insurance is needed, and that it is the landlord's responsibility to have the general buildings and insurance suitable for HMOs if that is the strategy. If possible, get a copy of the insurance to make sure it would not be in breach of the conditions.

You should also get professional indemnity insurance.

Top Ten Things That Can Go Wrong:

While it can happen in any aspect of property, rent-to-rent does seem particularly prone to things going wrong; but well-informed anticipation of potential problems can help, or, to coin a phrase:

Proper prior planning prevents poor performance!

Do not rush into this strategy without first considering the risks, such as these **top ten things that can go wrong:**

1. You pay too much to acquire a rent-to-rent deal

If you are paying finders' fees for a rent-to-rent deal, make sure the figures will work. I have seen deals offered where the finder's fee is six months or more of expected net rental profits – and that's before you've refurbished. Remember, this strategy is ALL about the cashflow and your contract with the owner is for a finite time with no guarantee of being extended.

The only way you might choose to pay relatively high finder's fees is with a view to paying to learn, so you can try out the strategy before committing time and expense to your own marketing efforts perhaps.

Ideally, you will find your own deals. Go back to the sourcing chapter for more about deal finding; most of it applies whether you are looking for rent-to-rent or purchase deals. Sourcing is the first and arguably most important skill that any property investor should develop.

2. The initial set up costs more or takes longer than expected

You must budget carefully and anticipate the costs involved. As mentioned earlier, you should not expect to pay for everything. The landlord should be prepared to assume responsibility for the boiler as well as other regulatory safety measures and external aspects of the property such as the roof. Make sure he understands this and has building insurance in place.

Re realistic in estimating costs or speak to others with more experience of refurbishment and the costs of adaptations that may be required to set up an HMO.

Get quotes from any tradesmen you anticipate needing and ask about their availability. Line up your team.

3. The property location turns out not to be good

It's important to work backwards from your goals. The first thing to consider is what area will work best for you, and this should include proximity to where you live as well as other factors such as the demand from your target tenant type and preferred model, including HMOs or short-term lets.

4. Voids are longer than anticipated, or rents are less

Don't just look at figures given to you by the person keen to charge you a finder's fee. Do your own due diligence.

Look on Rightmove, Spareroom, or, in the case of serviced accommodation, on Airbnb, Booking.com and other relevant sites to see what similar properties rent for by the room. Ask other local operators and find out how long they take to fill rooms.

5. The landlord tries to interfere or wants the property back

To minimise the risk of this, always meet the landlord or owner in person before entering into any agreement, so both parties can establish trust, whether you can get along and if a win-win deal can be struck. Be prepared to be open with each other and negotiate the heads of terms of the agreement to suit both parties.

6. The lender calls in the mortgage

There can be various reasons why a lender might call in a mortgage. The mortgage may be called in if the lender wants to repossess the property because the landlord has failed to make payments. Always make sure the lines of communication are open between the landlord and yourself and be prepared to come to some new agreement to prevent repossession taking place, such as buying the property below market value if possible.

If the landlord dies or goes bankrupt, any payments due to him by you could be put into an escrow account until such time as his affairs are settled.

7. A tenant or the landlord tries to sue you

Adequate insurance is vital as are robust contracts.

You should have professional indemnity insurance as mentioned earlier, and make sure that all eventualities you can possibly think of are covered one way or another by your insurance and your legal agreements with both the landlord and in the agreements with tenants.

8. Bad tenants trash the property

Think carefully upfront about what tenant type you want to target and be careful about the tenants you take on. I would advise using a tenant reference checking agency and contacting their previous landlord. If in any doubt, either don't take them on, or at least get guarantors. All the same, tenant checks should be done as if it were your own property.

9. You are not getting enough profit

Consider whether you could possibly get another lettable room out of the property. Is there a separate lounge or dining room that you hadn't thought of using at first? Or think about whether you could charge higher rents, maybe by changing the tenant type you're targeting; or try dressing your properties and taking better photographs for ads.

10. You simply can't cope

If you feel like you're all round just not coping, it could be time to get a mentor or seek further business advice.

It could be that better systems may help you to stay on top of your workload: try to analyse your processes and procedures and see where there's scope for improvement.

Are you delegating enough? Consider taking on staff if the profits are there to justify it, or outsource more. Maybe you could get a virtual PA, use more apps to help you get organised, or just develop a better filing system.

Risks and What Can Go Wrong for Landlords

As a landlord, you may be apprehensive about rent-to-rent. So, what can you do to protect yourself from incompetent or rogue operators?

Firstly, it's important to note that you as the landlord WILL ultimately be held liable for the property and the tenants' welfare should anything go wrong, either in terms of health and safety or any other rules and regulations breached, including any local authority HMO or other requirements, such as licensing or Article 4 directives (see HMOs Chapter 5 for further details).

Secondly, be careful when letting property that you're not being targeted by fraudsters who claim to want to rent your property themselves but secretly intend to use it for rent-to-rent (or any other purposes) without permission or compliance. If potential tenants offer to pay several months' rent upfront or above the rent being asked, alarms bells should be ringing.

Thirdly, be aware that many leasehold properties have covenants to prevent sub-letting, so such arrangements will be invalid. In the event, for instance, that a tenant is injured and seeks to sue the landlord, you will be held responsible. An example where this happened at a property let via Airbnb by a rent-to-rent operator is given by solicitor Giles Beaker in Chapter 6.

The only arrangements I have entered along the lines of rent-to-rent have been to lease properties to housing associations which has proven to be a good arrangement, relieving us of all the usual landlord hassles.

If you are happy to go ahead with any form of rent-to-rent, including guaranteed rent or leasing the property, do your due diligence on the operator in question and only deal with people who you can trust to offer a fully compliant and competent service, giving you peace of mind.

Further Reading, Resources and References

Jacquie Edwards has written two books about rent-to-rent:

- *Rent-to-Rent: Getting Started Guide*, Jacquie Edwards (Panoma Press, June 2017)

- *Rent-to-Rent: Your Questions Answered*, Jacquie Edwards (Panoma Press, Jun 2015)

Sarah Poynton-Ryan also teaches rent-to-rent at: https://www.onlinepropertycourses.com.

Neil McCoy-Ward is another trainer who has some good YouTube videos on the strategy: https://www.YouTube.com/watch?v=1pixJ1W7C2w&t=527s (copy the link or find online!)

Northwood Lettings & Estate Agents: http://www.northwooduk.com/pages/guaranteed-rent

National Approved Letting Scheme (NALS): http://www.nalscheme.co.uk/benefits-of-nals

Giles Beaker, partner at Anthony Gold solicitors: https://www.anthonygold.co.uk

How does this strategy appeal to you?

Rate this strategy, on a scale from 0 - 10, for the following factors:

0 . 1 . 2 . 3 . 4 . 5 . 6 . 7 . 8 . 9 . 10   **Time**

0 . 1 . 2 . 3 . 4 . 5 . 6 . 7 . 8 . 9 . 10   **Money**

0 . 1 . 2 . 3 . 4 . 5 . 6 . 7 . 8 . 9 . 10   **Risk**

0 . 1 . 2 . 3 . 4 . 5 . 6 . 7 . 8 . 9 . 10   **Appeal**

0 . 1 . 2 . 3 . 4 . 5 . 6 . 7 . 8 . 9 . 10   **Knowledge**

0 . 1 . 2 . 3 . 4 . 5 . 6 . 7 . 8 . 9 . 10   **Aptitude**

0 . 1 . 2 . 3 . 4 . 5 . 6 . 7 . 8 . 9 . 10   **Tax**

CHAPTER 4

BUY-TO-LET

*"Don't wait to buy property.
Buy property and wait!"*

An old saying

Introduction

This chapter is about straightforward, plain buy-to-let – sometimes known as *vanilla* buy-to-let. As this book covers many strategies, there is not scope to go into the same level of detail on buy-to-let as I wrote in my first book, *The Complete Guide to Property Investing Success*, which focused mainly on buy-to-let as it was to a large extent the only game in town at that time.

With government measures over the past few years to curb buy-to-let, there are more hurdles than ever to deal with, but that is not to say buy-to-let doesn't work anymore.

Do not be too easily put off this outstanding strategy for building wealth by the political pressures. Remember that decent private landlords provide homes for people who are either not in a position to buy at the present time or do not want to because they value the flexibility of renting.

Not all landlords will be affected by the tax changes set out in Section 24 (S24) of the Finance (no 2) Act 2015, limiting the amount of income tax relief higher rate landlords can get on residential property finance costs to the basic rate of income tax.

You will NOT be affected by S24 if:

- You are a basic rate 20% income tax payer (but check with your accountant that this will not change);

- Your properties are bought and owned in a limited company;

- You can move your properties into a limited company structure (see Chapter 11, Tax).

I still firmly believe that property is the best asset class there is, and I continue to invest and recommend it too. While it is good to consider other strategies, and be creative given the challenges facing investors today, buy-to-let is still the gold standard in my opinion. It is the most passive, no fuss and easiest way to invest in property. If you want to adopt the 'KISS' principle and keep it simple and straightforward, then buy-to-let is ideal.

So why bother with any other strategy? The fact is that it is harder today than it used to be, with higher prices, larger deposits and other factors such as the stamp duty surcharge on second homes and S24; as well as mortgage criteria being stricter.

A good overall strategy now, in my view, is to generate income from other strategies if you need to, then feed those profits into long-term buy-to-let. Buy some properties to sell for lump sums ideally too, to use as deposits for more buy-to-let property.

Show Me the Money

UK property is a great investment that has historically doubled in value every 7-12 years, and while not expected to increase in future at quite the same rate, is still set to continue growing over the long term. Expert predictions vary, but reports I have seen include a 50% increase in house prices by 2027 (from leading estate agent emoov.com) and prices doubling by 2030 (from Santander UK).

Let's look at an example of what could be achieved in five years, based on fairly average figures (£241,000 being the average house price in England at October 2017, www.ons.gov.uk) and property prices rising 5% per year:

Property purchase price £250,000

£250,000 + 5% value after 1 year = £262,500
After 2 years = £275,625
After 3 years = £289.406
After 4 years = £303,877
After 5 years = £319,070

Total increase in value = £69,000

Less stamp duty of £10,000* and Solicitors costs circa £1,500:

Figure includes the 3% stamp duty surcharge which affects everyone buying additional properties above £40,000; but it is a deductible capital expense against capital gains on selling.

Net gain after five years = £57,500

That's £11,500 per year of capital gains from just one property held for five years.

Now let's look at potential rental income:

Rent = £1,200 per month
Annual rent = £14,400 per year
Ongoing costs at 25%* per year = £3,600

*typical landlords' maintenance costs

Net rental income after costs = £10,800

The gross yield on the rent is determined by rent x 12 / purchase price:

£1,200 x 12 / £250,000 = 5.76%

This example is of an average property, with a purchase price of £250,000 and rental yield of 5.76%, that after just five years of growth at 5% per annum can deliver a net capital gain of £57,500.

Additionally, the property produces a net rental income of £10,800 per year: £54,000 over five years. The total capital and rental income is more than £100,000 in 5 years (or £111,500).

So, how many of these do you want?

Photo of a typical house of value @ £250,000 that we own locally.

The Leverage of Buy-to-Let Mortgages

Mortgages will be discussed at more length in Chapter 10 on Finance but it's important to mention here that many investors use mortgages as leverage, either through necessity or choice.

The fact is that buy-to-let mortgages have made it possible for many to invest in property to build portfolios. Prior to the advent of buy-to-let mortgages, the number of private landlords in the UK was very small. The Council of Mortgage Lenders (CML) record that lenders advanced more than 1.7 million buy-to-let loans between 1999 and 2015. Over the past 12 years the private rented sector has doubled in size. Buy-to-let mortgage balances outstanding recently grew to more than £200 billion.

The use of borrowed money, either by means of a buy-to-let mortgage or any other form of borrowing, enables you to buy more property. This leverage can greatly increase the return on investment (ROI) from the money you put in. It also magnifies your capital gains.

Following the example above, assuming you have £250,000 to invest, you could use the money to buy just one property with cash, or you could use it (*not including expenses for the sake of simplicity*) to put in four deposits of 25% and get 75% buy-to-let mortgages to buy four properties.

You now own not £250,000 but £1,000,000 worth of property.

Now, assuming the same growth rate of 5% per year, but having four properties due to leverage:

Property purchase price £250,000 x 4 = £1,000,000

£1,000,000 + 5%, value after 1 year = £1,050,000
After 2 years, value = £1,102,500
After 3 years, value = £1,157,625
After 4 years, value = £1,215,506
After 5 years, value = £1,276,281

Total increase in value = £276,281

You now have a gross capital gain of over a quarter of a million pounds at £276,281 in just five years, with values increasing just 5% per year (instead of a £69,000 gain from just one property).

This use of mortgages to magnify the returns on your investment is what makes buy-to-let so attractive.

The return on your investment (ROI) of £250,000 in this example has gone from 27.75% to well over 100% – more than 110% in fact.

Remember also, that buying four properties instead of just one means that you quadruple your rental income too. Of course, you will now have mortgage payments to make, and the tax implications applicable to your circumstances must also be considered.

Most of us enjoy thinking about the fantastic returns that may be possible from our investments, but we are buying real properties for real people to live in as tenants, so at some stage we need to move on from the spreadsheet to considering the reality of buy-to-let.

Below, we will consider the lifecycle of buy-to-let in terms of the various key stages you will encounter in your buy-to-let journey. If you want to get further into the nitty gritty of daily life for a self-managing landlord, you might like to read the excerpts from Dave's Diary included in Appendix IV, following the popularity of Dave's Diary in my first book. I also include a couple of entries in this chapter; as Dave likes to say, "Keep it real!"

Dave's Diary...

26th December:
Two call-outs from tenants on Boxing Day.

First call: "We have no lights, they've gone bang!" The tenants were not using the shower curtain and water had been splashed all over the floor and gone through the ceiling, tripping the fuse. Replaced the light fitting and told the tenants to use the shower curtain!

Second call: Tenants had no hot water. I found they were putting washing to air on top of the hot water tank which caused the immersion heater to cut out. I reset it and told them not to do that in future.

You also need to be aware of the many rules and regulations that exist in property…

Regulations

There are many rules and regulations in the business of renting property that we need to be aware of. I strongly suggest, particularly if you intend to self-manage, that you join a professional landlords' association as they are very good at giving advice and information about regulations. Both the National Landlords Association (NLA) and the Residential Landlords' Association (RLA) have a lot of useful information as well as telephone helplines. They also run events and courses relating to regulations and good practice for landlords. See contact details at the end of this chapter.

The Lifecycle of Buy-to-Let

So many things need to be considered when buying to let, it is useful to break it down in terms of the lifecycle of investing in stages, from:

- Choosing properties to buy;

- Deciding whether to buy locally or not;

- Preparing property to let;

- Getting tenants in;

- Should you self-manage?

- Ongoing management and maintenance;

- Ending the tenancy, eviction and pursuit of debts;

- Refurbishment;

- Selling up.

We will now look at each of these, in turn, for the remainder of the chapter.

Choosing Properties to Buy

How do you choose which property to buy? There are many factors to consider, such as location, type, whether you intend to self-manage; the yield and finance factors.

Firstly, it depends what you intend to do with the property. If you are purchasing as a project to refurbish and sell at a quick profit ('buying-to-sell'), you may look for different characteristics than if you are looking for a property to hold. When buying to sell the prime factors are whether you can buy sufficiently below market value and if there is scope to add value, as well as whether the market is strong enough to be assured of a timely sale.

If you are buying to let, other factors such as tenant demand become significant.

Unless it is a rural holiday home, the property should be in a reasonably built-up area and close enough to the town centre. It should also be of a size and type for which there is good tenant demand. You can check by asking agents and seeing what else is available online too. If you are unsure, you could place an advert for the type of property being considered (on Gumtree, for example) to see how many calls you get.

Also take into account how much work the property needs. If you need a mortgage, the lender will not allow you to buy property which is uninhabitable. It must have a working kitchen and bathroom and be ready to let within 30 days of purchase.

For buy-to-let, aim to strike a balance between buying a rundown property you can add value to, versus one that won't meet lender requirements and is too costly to refurbish. The location, value and potential rent will all be factors in how much money you should spend on it. As a rule, prime locations require prime refurbishments, décor and furnishings. Ensure the budget is appropriate for the property.

Service charges on flats can be quite high and eat into profits. Lease length can also affect value, so find out the estimated cost of a lease extension. We have found huge variations, some being relatively low-cost and others costing £25,000 or more.

I prefer freehold houses, but the price and other factors come into play, such as demographics: these days many live in smaller household units of one or two people, so don't need a three-bedroom house, and the rent for a house can exceed the budgets of many who are on benefits.

If you hope to rent to people on benefits, check that your mortgage lender allows it too. Some lenders do not, as families on benefits can be heavier on wear and tear and offer less security against damage (unless a suitable relative can act as a guarantor, which in practice landlords may require).

When you purchase a property, make sure your conveyancing solicitor puts your home address correctly on the Land Registry forms as this will help to protect you from property fraud. You can sign up free of charge to alerts of any activity on the title of your properties at Land Registry (see References section at the end of the chapter).

Deciding Whether to Buy Locally or Not

If you intend to self-manage, I suggest buying within 10 miles of where you live as a rule. We have sold properties that are further afield because they are just too much bother. Having said that, some of the properties we found most problematic were just a little too far away from our comfort zone – as Dave was trying to manage them but finding the travel time an issue.

We have several non-local properties that are 200 miles away and more which I manage without agents. I am lucky to have good tenants who are understanding that I can't get there and who help to find trusted tradesmen. Works are generally more expensive of course. I had one instance where a toilet needed fixing and I was charged £400. Dave, on the other hand, bought a new toilet for a local property that he fitted himself, at a cost of £40. On balance, as it has proved expensive, I now sell non-local properties when they become empty.

Some investors who live in expensive areas choose to buy in cheaper areas, usually in a south to north direction. As a general rule, prices tend to be lower the further away from London in any direction, while rental returns (yields) are higher.

Other reasons for buying non-locally include investing in student property near to a university, some buying where their children go to university.

Hotspots:

A hotspot is a term used for any area in favour, normally where prices are doing particularly well, but other factors can come into play too. Some favour areas with cheap properties under £40,000 that are not subject to the 3% stamp duty surcharge. High prices and low yields in London and the south are leading more investors to investigate cheaper parts of the country.

With a view to buying for the long term, I am not inclined to be led by hotspots as it can be a short-term phenomenon; or by high yields non-locally which don't necessarily translate into good net returns. Overall, we prefer to buy locally.

Preparing Property to Let

An energy performance certificate (EPC) is a legal requirement for any property today on sale (or purchase). This must be available from the time of purchase and before letting, and a copy must be made available to tenants. Note that if the property requires refurbishment, a new EPC may be needed to reflect works done that may affect the rating, such as a new heating system or windows.

Any properties rated as an F or a G on the energy efficiency rankings, the lowest possible ratings, need to be upgraded for new tenancies as from April 2018 and for existing tenancies by 2020.

Health and safety is an important general principle that must be adhered to in rental properties and every local council has a department dedicated to ensuring the principles are applied. They can help with information about their requirements, and this is especially important for houses in multiple occupation (HMOs). Make sure your property is safe and free from health hazards and keep it in a good state of repair. Your professional landlords' association can also help if there is anything you are unsure about.

Gas safety: Landlords must have an annual gas safety check carried out by a gas safe registered engineer and provide tenants with a copy of the Landlords' Gas Safety Certificate.

Fire safety: the rules on fire safety vary depending on whether your property is in England, Wales, Scotland or Northern Ireland regarding smoke alarms and carbon monoxide alarms but should always be adhered to. Further information is freely available from several sources including councils, professional landlords' associations, gov.uk and of course the fire service.

Houses in Multiple Occupation (HMOs) will have specific rules for fire alarm systems which must be checked regularly, and for means of escape (such as stairs and landings) which must remain unobstructed.

While annual electrical checks in single-let properties are not currently required, landlords must nevertheless ensure the electrical wiring and all electric appliances are safe. HMOs must have a periodic inspection carried out every five years by a suitably qualified electrician.

Getting Tenants In

There is more to getting tenants into your rental property than simply placing an advert and moving them in! Rules and regulations apply every step of the way. Not getting it right can get you into trouble with the local council or on the wrong side of the law and could even make it difficult to evict should you subsequently need to.

The first thing to think about is what sort of tenants you are prepared to rent to. This will have a bearing on where you advertise or search for tenants.

As with everything in property, things continually change, and it is important to keep your knowledge up to date. For example, regarding the roll-out of universal credit:

Benefit Tenants and Universal Credit

First introduced in 2013, this system was designed to roll up various benefits, including housing benefit, into a single payment that could only be paid direct to one person in a household. The implication for investors was that rent would no longer be paid direct to the landlord except in exceptional cases that need to be agreed. Many landlords say they will not accept tenants on universal credit.

Before universal credit, for many years our local niche strategy was letting to tenants on housing benefit, the Local Housing Allowance (LHA). This worked well when rents achievable were higher than for working tenants. Later, the way in which the LHA rate was calculated led to this difference being eroded but we continued with benefit tenants because we had a good relationship with the local council, who would do all the necessary pre-let checks and had a deposit guarantee scheme, which all made our lives easier.

However, eventually the differential in rents was turned on its head and higher rents could now be achieved by renting to private tenants. We resisted the change as it was in our comfort zone to stick with the LHA tenants and the council's support, but when the government changed the tax rules we knew that we needed to be fair to ourselves and had to abandon this sector of the market as it just wasn't profitable any more. The recent introduction of universal credit in our area has further discouraged us from operating in the benefits sector.

Professional working tenants

We have started letting to professional working tenants and use a letting agent zoom995.co.uk who offer a very good and reasonably priced tenant-find-only service (for finding and checking-in tenants).

Landlords in England are now required to check the ID of all prospective adult tenants to make sure they can legally rent your property. This is one of the reasons we use an agent for tenant-find as they will do this for you. If in doubt, get help or ask the NLA or RLA.

The assured shorthold tenancy (AST), or in Scotland short assured tenancy agreement, sets out the expectations and legally binding obligations of both landlord and tenant, with a fixed term normally of six months (minimum) to a year. After that, it reverts to a 'periodic tenancy' unless you renew the fixed term. It is easier to evict if necessary once the tenancy is outside the fixed term.

While not obligatory, an inventory is definitely worthwhile for your own protection in case of counter claims by the tenant, should you need to withhold deposit monies for damages during the tenancy. Whether you compile the inventory yourself or get an independent inventory clerk to do one, make sure it is comprehensive and completed before or on the day of check in. Again, any good letting agent should arrange this for you even for a tenant-find-only service.

Deposit protection: you must place or insure your tenant's deposit in a government authorised tenancy deposit protection scheme within 30 days of receiving the deposit.

At the start of a new tenancy, you must give tenants:

- a copy of the government's *How to Rent Guide* if you live in England (find at gov.uk);

- a "tenant information pack" in Scotland (find at www.gov.scot/ publications).

Utilities: Remember to read the gas and electric meters before tenants move in (and water meter if any) and get the utilities and council tax bills put in the tenant's name, unless the property is an HMO with tenants on different contracts.

Should You Self-Manage?

This is a very central question. Let's face it, when you buy property, your eye is normally on the prize of capital gains and the yield of rental income. You are not doing it to sign up for fixing toilets or arguing with tenants about the rent. But someone has to do the work. The question is, could it be you, or if not, can you afford to pay others to do the work and what will you do with your time instead?

Some people believe quite passionately that you should not be involved in the nitty gritty, arguing that if you put a high value on your time, why would you paint walls or clean property when you could pay someone just £10 an hour to do so? As a self-managing landlord, Dave would say in response that it is never as simple as that.

For one thing, it is about focus. By managing your properties personally, you are keeping a close eye on them. I do think Dave's properties are like his babies. Yes, you could send your baby to nursery and pay others to look after them, just as you could pay others to look after your properties, but you might get great satisfaction out of taking on this role yourself.

Dave's Diary...

12th December:

Replaced some window hinges at 31B as the windows weren't shutting properly. I get hinges from Screwfix @ £5 - £10, after measuring for what size required. You have to take the window out to remove the old hinges and fix the new ones. Windows can be quite heavy and it's an awkward job detaching and catching the window, so get someone to help if possible.

You will find lots of videos for jobs like this on YouTube if you don't know how to do it.

In any case, self-managing a large portfolio is basically our full-time focus and way of life. It may not always take up the hours of a full-time job, but it varies and can be full-on. It is a big commitment to always be available for the tenants and the properties. We do not 'need' to self-manage our properties at this stage from a financial point of view, but Dave enjoys the work as he is very practical and good at doing the maintenance. He has a background in engineering.

Crucially as well, as Dave says, he "has no imagination" and would not otherwise make great plans. That is often one of the central arguments against self-managing – that you could otherwise be busy on plans to make more money than you save by doing the work; but the argument only holds true if you would do, otherwise it's just rhetoric.

The other thing is, by handing over control to others, there is always a risk of things being done badly or that you could be ripped off by tradesmen or even rogue agents. Dave likes to be in control. I'm not saying I always necessarily agree with his perspective – especially when I'm being asked to help with cleaning; but it does not have to be a black-and-white argument, a once-and-for-all unchanging decision – there can be shades of grey. We recently found a young man who is a great help and now does most of the painting at our properties for us.

I self-manage some of my non-local properties in the sense of not employing letting agents on an ongoing basis, even though I cannot do the maintenance and it would be impractical for Dave to do, being 200 miles away. This works most of the time although it does reduce profits as I must pay for all work to be done by others. If you are managing this way, you should at least be reachable during normal office hours so that you can respond to tenant issues and enquiries promptly.

Ongoing Management and Maintenance

Most estimates of the average maintenance costs for properties are thought to be anywhere from 25% - 40% but our costs typically sit at 12% - 15%, as Dave does most of the maintenance.

We do use professional tradesmen but keep this to a minimum. Here is a list of the trades we most frequently use:

- Gas safe engineer to carry out annual Landlords Gas Safety Inspections and issue certificates; boiler repairs and replacement; occasionally a whole new heating system.

- Electricians as required.

- Double glazing man: to replace windows where the seal has gone; windows broken; old windows that need replacing; sometimes whole house including doors.

- Roofer: many of our houses happen to have a small flat roof area over the front porch and sometimes entrance areas which need attention.

- Painter & Decorator: recently we have someone help with painting and decorating as there has been so much activity with the number of properties being sold.

Here are some things we commonly do ourselves (mainly Dave but I help when I can):

- Cleaning.

- Clearing overgrown gardens, often left full of rubbish (I often help with gardens too).

- Getting rid of rubbish – sometimes whole housefuls, in which case we may get help!

- Fixing and repairing things: Dave is very good at fixing things, having an engineering background.

- Carpet fitting: Dave fits carpets himself most of the time, buying usually from Carpetright and delivering them to the property on the roof rack of his car. Occasionally we get them to fit carpets for an extra professional finish or in awkward spaces.

- Unblocking drains: it can be very expensive to use companies like Dyno-Rod. Instead, Dave has drain rods that he uses himself after trying chemical treatment and other investigations first; this works nine times out of ten, otherwise the professional companies can send cameras down to investigate serious blockages.

- Ladder work: gutters, etc – Dave is not afraid to go up a ladder and clean or fix gutters and such. Again, the occasional big job may warrant paying others to do the work.

Doing your own maintenance can save you a fortune (assuming you are good at it). Dave says: *"It's important to have the right infrastructure: the right tools, car or van, and storage facilities."* We have several garages where we store things (both at home and garages in blocks that came with properties we bought that we do not let with the property). Dave has an estate car with a roof rack which is more versatile than a van as he often carries things on the roof rack as well as in the car.

Dave carries tools as well as spare lightbulbs and other frequently needed things (including fillers and sealants caulk, sanitary sealant and Fixall which can even be used on wet surfaces), a cordless LED inspection lamp, an extension lead, work gloves, knee pads, a cordless drill, smoke alarm batteries, fuses, fuse wire, tap washers, fibre washers, float valve seals, ceiling pendants and light pendant skirts, screws and nails, nuts and bolts, rawlplugs… As he was telling me this, I said we'd better stop now or we'll end up with a Screwfix catalogue-full, but that's the gist of it!

Ending the Tenancy, Eviction and Pursuit of Debts

When ending a tenancy, particularly under difficult or adverse circumstances (such as non-payment of rent), you must follow the correct legal procedures, even if the fixed term of the tenancy has expired.

Here are some of the forms you will need:

You must first serve tenants with a Section 21 giving two months' notice ending on a rent day, then you can apply for a possession order using a form N5b and get a certificate of service, N215. When you get your possession order, to enforce it you need a bailiffs' warrant (if they don't leave by the date of possession) which can be applied for using form N325.

If you want to pursue ex-tenants for debts, use the high court sheriffs who also offer a tracing facility. First you need a high court writ which the sheriffs will get for you, then you can ask them to trace the people (both costs can be added to what the tenants owe, although you will have to pay those costs if attempts to find them are unsuccessful).

You can't exercise a S21 during the term of a tenancy, so instead you need to use a S8 in which case you need to cite grounds and there will be a court hearing during which you'll be asked to prove that they've done what you said they did. Dave has been to court with neighbours' evidence of anti-social behaviour, but the tenant can appeal, and the judge could change the judgment. In this case, the judge overturned his own earlier decision when the tenant appealed.

Tenants can also appeal against a S21, but that judgment is irreversible. The hearing could still take place and Dave has had this, but the judge will not overturn the judgment.

The council have at times intervened to make an emergency discretionary housing payment on behalf of tenants to sustain the tenancy and prevent eviction.

If you apply for possession using a S8 (which is why we have 6-month tenancies), you use a form N5, also form N119 (both together) and also N215 (certificate of service). Same N325 as for a bailiffs' warrant.

Use form N1 to sue someone for money – to apply for a judgment of money owed. Use County Court Bailiffs to enforce, or High Court Sheriffs. Dave normally uses County Court Bailiffs to evict (or get money from) tenants still living at the property, and High Court Sheriffs for tracing tenants after they've left and not given a forwarding address – to trace and then enforce High Court Writs for money owed, as the Sheriffs persist more on such matters.

Here is a table of the various forms, what they are for and current costs:

Current Fee	What You Want	Form To Get	Form To Enforce	Current Fee
£355	Possession (S21)	N5B & N215	N325	£121 (CCB*)
£355	Possession (S8)	N5 & N119 & N215	N325	£121 (CCB)
£ varies	Money Claim	N1	N323	£ varies
£66	High Court Writ	(the Sheriffs deal with)	-	-
£ varies	Tracing service	(the Sheriffs deal with)	-	-
		High Court Sheriffs are like bailiffs but private firms.		*CCB = County Court Bailiffs

Refurbishment

Over the course of the lifetime of owning a property it may need refurbishment more than once. If you buy a run-down property to secure a bargain, you will need to refurbish the property in preparation to get it ready to rent. You may need to refurbish between lets too.

When refurbishing to let or re-let, we aim to be practical and frugal. *"We're in the business of making money here!"* Dave likes to say. But when we are getting ready to sell, presentation becomes key to maximising the price achievable, and "style over substance", as Dave says, is for once allowed.

We do sometimes sell properties without refurbishment – it's a judgment call you need to make for each property and will depend on a variety of factors such as:

- How 'hot' the local market is at the time of sale. I once bought a property in Cambridge that was in a bad state and it was not the only one I viewed like that. The market was so hot that sellers often didn't bother making any effort. In fact buyers would fight over properties in need of work, on the assumption of finding at least something of a bargain.

- The condition of the property when vacated by tenants – sometimes they are left in a good clean state with no work necessary.

- How remote the property is from you and the practicalities of organising the refurb – although it can be done and I've personally stayed over many a time at non-local properties to help with refurbishments.

Here are some average costs for common refurbishment works on a 3-bed house to give you an example of typical costs. These represent roughly what we have typically paid for such works:

Works Required	Average Cost Estimates (we paid)
New kitchen	£3,500
New bathroom	£3,500
Complete new central heating system	£4,000
Replace all double glazing inc pvc doors	£5,000
Carpets throughout	£800
Painting and decorating if paying someone to do	£750
Rubbish removal (where quite a substantial amount)	£200

Selling

While buy-to-let is certainly a long-term strategy, the time can come for a variety of reasons when it is right to sell. Why sell, what, where and when?

We have sold some of our properties in order to realise capital gains which enabled us to help our children and to reduce our mortgage gearing from 75% to 50%, in response to the S24 tax changes mentioned earlier. We also moved some into a limited company, but this was not cost-effective for most of the properties due to large capital gains.

We had to decide what to sell and when. We decided to start selling as properties became empty and found this happening naturally at a rate of about one a month which suited us as it spreads the workload and keeps cashflow smoother than selling multiple properties at once.

More recently, we decided to stop selling local 3-bed houses, and only sell flats from now on. We are taking the opportunity to rebalance and *cull* the portfolio and improve its overall quality.

On the question of where: I have favoured selling non-local properties because they are more expensive to maintain.

"Never sell" is advice I have often heard with regard to property, and years ago I may have been inclined to agree; but I now see that it is not always that simple. None of us foresaw the many changes to tax and other regulations that have made landlords have to rethink and in some cases restructure. I have learned that it is always necessary to keep knowledge current and to be prepared to adapt and change.

Many landlords, like ourselves, who got into buy-to-let early, are now in their 50s, and while we are still blessed with good health, the future needs careful and realistic planning and there may come a time when we no longer want to own the properties. Thinking ahead even further, estate planning and inheritance are matters that will be looked at further in Chapter 11, on Tax.

Further Reading, Resources and References

Book: *The Complete Guide to Property Investing Success*, by Angela Bryant (Dec 2008, Panoma Press)

Emoov.com property price predictions can be found at www.emoov.co.uk/news

Santander property predictions can be found at www.santander.co.uk

Council of Mortgage Lenders (CML) www.cml.org.uk

Sign up for free fraud alerts at https://propertyalert.landregistry.gov.uk

National Landlords' Association: www.landlords.org.uk

Residential Landlords' Association: www.rla.org.uk

For information about Energy Performance Certificates: www.epcregister.com

For information about Landlords; Gas Safety Certificates: www.gassaferegister. co.uk

Agents we use for tenant-find-only and also for property sales: www.zoom995. co.uk

Right to rent: https://www.gov.uk/check-tenant-right-to-rent-documents

Tenant deposit protection: https://www.gov.uk/tenancy-deposit-protection

How does this strategy appeal to you?

Rate this strategy, on a scale from 0 - 10, for the following factors:

0 . 1 . 2 . 3 . 4 . 5 . 6 . 7 . 8 . 9 . 10   **Time**

0 . 1 . 2 . 3 . 4 . 5 . 6 . 7 . 8 . 9 . 10   **Money**

0 . 1 . 2 . 3 . 4 . 5 . 6 . 7 . 8 . 9 . 10   **Risk**

0 . 1 . 2 . 3 . 4 . 5 . 6 . 7 . 8 . 9 . 10   **Appeal**

0 . 1 . 2 . 3 . 4 . 5 . 6 . 7 . 8 . 9 . 10   **Knowledge**

0 . 1 . 2 . 3 . 4 . 5 . 6 . 7 . 8 . 9 . 10   **Aptitude**

0 . 1 . 2 . 3 . 4 . 5 . 6 . 7 . 8 . 9 . 10   **Tax**

CHAPTER 5

HOUSES IN MULTIPLE OCCUPATION (HMOs)

"Some people dream of success, while others wake up and work hard at it."

Wayne Huizenga

In the last chapter we looked at plain or 'vanilla' buy-to-let, renting whole properties to a single household or family unit. Many investors seek to increase income by letting properties by the room as houses in multiple occupation (HMOs), the subject of this chapter. An HMO property is variously referred to as a 'multi-let', 'house share' or 'shared accommodation'.

Definition of HMO

An HMO is broadly defined as a property rented out by at least three people who form more than one household (see below) but share facilities like the bathroom and kitchen. The definition can be extended to blocks of converted flats too, where the communal areas are shared.

My brother Antony and I bought the property shown below as a development project and converted it into seven self-contained flats which we let out. The building itself is classified as an HMO even though the individual flats are let singly, and requires an HMO licence. Defining HMOs can get quite complex in such cases. The Residential Landlords Association (RLA) provides a good source of further information on this (see the references at the end of this chapter).

Photo: Rhyl property classed as HMO, although arranged as
seven self-contained flats let singly.

What is a household?

The following are considered households for the purposes of the Housing Act 2004:

- Couples who are married to each other or living together (and equivalent relationships for same sex couples);

- Relatives living together, including parents, grandparents, children (and step children), grandchildren, brothers, sisters, uncles, aunts, nephews and nieces or cousins;

- Half-relatives are treated the same as full relatives; and a foster child living with foster parents is treated as living in the same household as the foster parents.

In our early days, Dave and I bought a house that was already operating as an HMO, and agreed to allow the current tenants to stay. It was in an area that did not attract students or professionals and was occupied by men who were out of work and on benefits. There were several worrying incidents at the property but mostly it just took up an inordinate amount of Dave's time and put us off having HMOs, so we happily found our niche in mainly single lets.

Nevertheless, HMOs represent a great way to increase rental returns, with careful management and thought about how to structure your business for growth, should you want. I think it is especially good for people who may only have one or two properties yet who **do** have the time to manage them effectively. See **Dan's Story** later in the chapter.

Getting a mortgage for an HMO should be reasonably straightforward, assuming you would be eligible for a buy-to-let mortgage. There are fewer products and more questions will be asked about the property set-up, but don't let this put you off. This will be discussed further in Finance, Chapter 10.

Comparing HMO Income With BTL

For landlords, of course, the attraction of HMOs is the higher income relative to single lets, but renting by the room can also be attractive for tenants, being somewhat cheaper for them.

Here for comparison is an example of the saving for tenants on renting a room versus a self-contained one-bed flat, based on the current LHA rates in our local area:

Size of Accommodation	Weekly Amount	Monthly Amount	Annual Amount
Shared Accommodation	£79.55	£344.72	£4,136.60
One bedroom (self-contained)	£151.50	£656.50	£7,878.00
One bed costs more than room	**£71.95**	**£311.78**	**£3,741.40**

As you can see, the cost is almost double for a self-contained one-bedroom property. Given that anyone under 35 (unless with children) will not be eligible for the one-bedroom rate, they are especially likely to prefer an HMO.

The table below shows the rates in the same area for two, three and four-bedroom properties arranged as either single lets or HMOs. Assuming you could get three rooms from a two-bed property (where possible), four rooms from a three-bed and six from a four-bed (in practice three and four-bed houses can vary a lot in size and scope), the table shows examples of how much more gross rent could be achievable through letting the properties as HMOs:

Size of Accommodation	Weekly Amount	Monthly Amount	Single Let Annual Amount	HMO total x rooms, annual amount	Higher Gross Income HMOs over Single Lets
2 bed property, or as 3 bed HMO	£185.81	£805.18	£9,662.12	£12,409.80	£2,747.68
3 bed property, or as 4 bed HMO	£222.54	£964.34	£11,572.08	£16,546.40	£4.974.32
4 bed property, or as 6 bed HMO	£309.67	£1,341.90	£16,102.84	£24,819.60	£8,716.76

In practice, it may be possible to create even more lettable rooms in the case of larger properties, giving an even greater differential in the returns possible from HMOs.

In contrast, any property larger than a modest sized three or four-bedroom house is likely to give insufficient yield as a single let, making it unviable in most cases **except** as an HMO. Such larger properties should always be considered for either multi-lets or conversion to self-contained flats.

The greater gross returns from HMOs may appear to make it an obvious choice over single let buy-to-lets, but it is important to be realistic about the greater costs involved in both setting up and running HMOs, not to mention the extra time and management required.

Setting the property up as an HMO can also involve a longer void at the outset, as there is more work to be done, such as fitting fire doors. Additionally, while it is quite normal to offer single-let properties as unfurnished, HMOs are usually offered fully furnished – extra time and expense.

HMO landlords should also expect to pay utilities, at least up to a certain level if not entirely. Here is an example of the gross and net rental income from an HMO.

Example of Gross and Net Rental Income from HMO vs Single Let

These figures are for a 5-bedroom HMO, based on the room rates as shown earlier. Here is a breakdown of typical running costs:

Electricity £100.00
Gas £110.00
Water £65.00
Council Tax £90.00
Broadband £30.00
TV £12.25
Insurance £22.75

Monthly total costs: £430.00
Annual costs: £5,160.00

Monthly rent £1,723.60
Annual Rent £20,683.20

15% allowance for maintenance and voids £3,102.48

(a greater allowance than for single lets)

NET ANNUAL INCOME as an HMO: £17,580.72

The same property as a single let would achieve gross annual income of just £11,572.08*

*Based on the same rates for the area given above.

With a 10% allowance for maintenance and voids of £1,157.21

NET ANNUAL INCOME as a single let: £10,414.87

From these figures, you can see that the income from HMOs can be substantially higher than from single lets.

Especially if you have just a few properties, it can be a great way to maximise your income from them. Take my friend, Dan, who was made redundant at the age of 57 and used his redundancy money to buy just two HMOs. His preference was to have a small portfolio, as he explains.

Dan's Story

In 2012 I was made redundant at the age of 57, with a reasonable redundancy package but little hope of future professional employment on a par with my career to date, due to my age and changes in the industry.

Prior to this, our household expenditure – with four children to support – was around £5,000 per month, my wife earning just £12,000 per year. I realised we would have to limit our spending to £2,000 a month from now on and cut out holidays etc. I also worked out that the money would only last about 12 years, so I had to think of a way to earn money.

Knowing Angela and her brother Antony, both in property, led me to wonder if property could be the way forward. I got involved in helping with refurbs when I could, working for free to learn the ropes. At the same time, I tried various other ideas to see what might work. I also read Rich Dad, Poor Dad by Robert Kiyosaki, which helped me to understand the entrepreneurial and property mindset further after a lifetime of being employed.

Eventually, I decided upon HMOs, after crunching the numbers carefully and comparing them to single lets. Student lettings were something we had experience of as parents of children at university and we knew that we could provide a better standard through hard work and determination than the average student accommodation that we had seen.

In considering location, we looked first at high-level factors such as the university itself, the local authority rules and the cost of property in the areas considered. We made a short-list.

We then thought about practical issues such as carrying out and / or supervising works at the property, then decided it would be best to buy not too far from home – and near to a university where one of our children had attended. We felt we knew the type of students that the university attracted and the typical families, which made us feel more comfortable.

We looked into the supply and demand factors which were all positive, and it helped that, through friends, I knew several youngsters aiming to go to the university. We met with the university accommodation officer who gave us a lot of useful tips and said that student choice boils down to two things: proximity and price.

My wife took charge of choosing the actual property to buy, which would fulfil all the required criteria and be suitable for conversion to a 4-bed HMO within the target area and in line with all the local authority rules and regulations.

I considered scaling up as quickly as possible using all the mortgage leverage I possibly could, but found that lenders were not willing to lend, as I was just starting out with no earnings from a job or any track record in property. They wanted to see accounts and experience, so I just bought one with cash at first.

We ran the single HMO for 18 months, then used a mortgage broker to find a mortgage to enable us to buy a second one.

Costings for the work required dictated that we do as much as possible ourselves. I was lucky to have contacts of tradespeople through family who could be trusted to do the work I couldn't do myself, for a good price and in a timely manner.

Once the work of setting the property up was complete, letting the house was easy because the university had a website that was free to use for landlords who had been certified by the local authority as compliant with their standards and those of the university.

The only mistake we made was who we let the property to – big mistake! We took the first to view, an all-male group, without checking them out carefully, and they did not treat the place with the respect we had hoped for after all our hard work. But we lived and learned and got better students in subsequent years!

I thoroughly enjoy my building maintenance work and keeping our student HMOs to a high standard:

- *We work on our houses every July, doing compliance, remedial and improvement works.*

- *There is an Annual Accommodation Fair, which needs attendance and follow-up, which is our main marketing tool.*

- *There is a Student Accommodation website, which needs to be kept up to date and helps with marketing, especially if we do not fully let via the Annual Accommodation Fair.*

- *We cut the grass and do basic weekly maintenance one day per week, throughout the year.*

- *We respond as quickly as possible to requests from tenants for repairs and always do as good a job as we can with good quality materials.*

I feel confident that even if a build-to-rent corporation entered the local student market, we could find another tenant group for our properties to rent to, as it's a good area with plenty of demand for good properties.

I hope you enjoyed Dan's story, which highlights the fact that HMOs can be a good alternative to vanilla buy-to-let for those keen to achieve greater cashflow.

Remember that when you first set up an HMO there will be extra work and expense. Here is a list of fairly common works. This should be read in conjunction with any rules and guidance you receive from the local authority:

- Fitting fire doors;

- Locks on doors;

- Furnishing;

- Your HMO may need soundproofing;

- Extra showers and washing facilities;

- High speed internet connections.

Rules and Regulations for HMOs

This section of the chapter is concerned with the various levels and types of rules and regulations that apply to HMOs, of which there are many, both national and local. The central government site at gov.uk gives extensive guidance regarding the national rules, while it is very important to look also at the rules of your local council (ie the council local to the property).

The exact definition and rules for HMOs also vary between England, Scotland and Wales and you should be aware of the applications for the location of your property.

Local councils can apply rules further to the national guidelines regarding minimum room sizes and other basic requirements, like amount of worktop space per person in kitchens. They can also impose further HMO licensing requirements as discussed below.

Rules and restrictions on HMOs will be applied in various ways, through:

- Licensing;

- Health & Safety requirements;

- Planning permission, Use Class and Article 4;

- Building regulations.

Each of these components of HMO regulation will now be looked at in turn.

Licensing

A large HMO will always require a licence. The property will be defined as a large HMO if all the following apply:

- It is rented to 5 or more people who form more than 1 household;

- It is at least 3 storeys high;

- Tenants share toilet, bathroom or kitchen facilities.

HMO Licences are generally issued for five years and may cost from £100 to £1,400 or more a year, depending on the area. Some local councils calculate the charge per property, others per room.

At the time of writing the government is considering proposals to require all HMOs of five or more people to have a licence even if only on 2 storeys, instead of the current 3-storey requirement, meaning that more HMOs will need a licence.

If the property does require a licence, the local authority will do checks to ensure it complies with all their requirements such as having sufficient space for the tenants, health & safety requirements and so on, as further discussed below. The exact requirements vary from one council to another and are subject to change, so you must find out the requirements from your local council. The standards required for licensable HMOs are stricter and higher than for smaller HMOs that do not require a licence.

Only larger HMOs require a Mandatory HMO Licence (under The Housing Act, 2004). However, local councils have the power to impose Additional or Selective Licensing:

Mandatory Licensing (UK-wide): Is required for HMOs of 3 or more storeys with five or more people living over 3 storeys or more and forming more than one household.

Additional Licensing (Local councils can apply): Could be required where 3 - 6 individuals live in a 2-storey or even single-storey property. This may be applied city-wide or only in designated areas.

Selective Licensing (also decided by local authorities): Can be required of individual landlords, who may be selectively required to have a licence for all their rental properties.

In Wales, all landlords have to be licenced for any HMOs.

Failure to obtain a licence where one is required can lead to fines of up to £20,000. You would also not be able to legally serve a Section 21 notice to start the process of evicting a tenant should you need to do so. In addition, tenants could reclaim up to 12 months' rent.

Health and Safety

If your HMO requires a licence, your local council will advise on everything you need to do in terms of health and safety requirements for obtaining the licence and to ensure tenants' safety.

All the normal buy-to-let requirements apply, such as annual gas safety checks.

Additional requirements may include:

- An Electrical Installation Condition Report. This applies to **all** HMOs, not just licenced ones, and must be carried out every five years.

- Your HMO may need soundproofing.

- Fire safety: You may need or wish to speak to your local Fire Safety Officer about the requirements.

Planning Permission, Use Class and Article 4

In formal and legislative terms, different "use classes" exist for different types of property and this affects what you can use the property for, or do to it.

- A standard single-family home has the Use Class C3;

- An HMO (of up to 6 people) has the Use Class C4.

Under current national legislation, you do not normally need planning permission for a change of use class to convert a family home to an HMO, as this by default comes under the banner of 'permitted development'. However, local councils can adopt an Article 4 Direction which removes the automatic right to certain types of 'permitted development' such as this change of use class, making it necessary to obtain planning permission before you can do so.

Not all councils impose an Article 4 directive, and in areas where they do, it may be applied only to certain parts of the city or area. Often this is done to limit the number of HMOs where the local council consider that the presence of (more) HMOs would have a negative impact on the area. It is unlikely that planning permission will be forthcoming in such areas, given that Article 4 is brought in to limit the proliferation of HMOs.

Planning permission is always required for larger HMOs that house more than six people. Applying for planning permission can be complex and you may prefer your architect, solicitor or builder to submit the application on your behalf; or use a professional planning consultant.

When you are buying a property with the intention of creating an HMO, you need to know whether the area has Article 4 restrictions. Even if it does not, it is worth asking other landlords about their experiences. Also ask your professional landlords association and most importantly ask the local council, even take professional advice if necessary.

If planning permission is required, it will take time, and so your cashflow will be affected. It could be difficult to get lending in such circumstances.

Building Regulations

When you undertake any work to your HMO property, you must speak to your local council regarding their building regulations policy first and get approval if required, otherwise they could disallow works and require them to be undone.

You may be unclear as to how the planning and building regulations regimes differ. This is from www.planningportal.co.uk:

> *"Planning departments seek to guide the way our towns, cities and countryside develop. This includes the use of land & buildings, the appearance of buildings, landscaping considerations, highway access and the impact that the development will have on the general environment.*
>
> *While building regulations set standards for the design and construction of buildings to ensure the safety and health for people in or about those*

buildings. They also include requirements to ensure that fuel and power is conserved, and facilities are provided for people, including those with disabilities, to access and move around inside buildings.

For many types of building work, separate permission under both regimes (separate processes) will be required. For other building work, such as internal alterations, buildings regulations approval will probably be needed, but planning permission may not be. If you are in any doubt you should contact your local planning authority or a building control body."

Local authorities work with universities to enforce building regulations, often making conversion costs higher but producing a better product.

Choosing Property to Buy for HMO

If you are choosing a property to set up as an HMO, you need to consider the suitability of the size and layout. You need to be aware of the rules regarding minimum room sizes both nationally and locally. A three-bedroom terraced house with a small open-plan lounge and tiny third bedroom may not be suitable to house more than three people and as such will not be profitable as an HMO.

Some three-bedroom properties, even terraced, can be suitable – it depends on the layout. If there is a separate lounge that can be converted to a bedroom and an adequately sized third bedroom, with maybe even a downstairs toilet, that is a much better proposition. In some cases, there may even be scope to install a downstairs shower room, which is ideal (as long as you can make the numbers stack!).

Even in some larger properties, the layout could be such as to require too much work to adapt, making them unsuitable choices compared to others with a more suitable layout where the costs would be much lower.

A double-fronted Victorian house with stairs that rise in the middle, like our property in Rhyl shown earlier, for example, lends itself much better to conversion than a property which might have the stairs to one side that would need to be moved at great expense and new corridors created to split a property into apartments as we did in Rhyl.

Should you provide a communal area?

Opinions vary among landlords on this matter, but it seems to be generally agreed that while it's good to provide some communal space such as a decent-sized kitchen-diner, it is not necessary to forgo making a separate lounge into a potential bedroom for example which would add little value to tenants while unacceptably reducing the property's profitability. Many councils provide guidance to landlords and potential landlords on this important matter. If you are thinking of entering the student market, universities may have additional rules that need to be observed.

Location and Targeting Tenant Type

Deciding where to buy your HMO should go hand in hand with deciding the tenant type to target. If you want to rent to students, the property should be as near as possible to the university or college where they study. If you want to rent to professionals, consider being close to a tube station in London and general amenities including good transport links elsewhere.

Student Lets

It is worth giving further thought to renting to students. Here are some tips for renting to students from Dan whose story was shared earlier:

- Start with the University Accommodation Office and local council – their website will let you know about their HMO rules and Article 4 or any "Consultation process" which is ongoing.

- Proximity and price are the two overriding principles that govern students' choices. Make sure you know whether the university has multiple sites or one campus.

- Never believe property sellers who say that their property is suitable for students – check.

- Get your costings and projections right before you take your first step.

- Your long-term plans could be scuppered by large developers building accommodation villages near to the university, so always have an exit plan that allows you to sell the property as a family home, or to recycle into another HMO model.

- You must always have a guarantor.

- Get to know the contract laws and norms specific to this niche area – whilst students and their parents rarely read contracts, some parents do and you must.

- Some universities have Security Patrol Schemes or their own local "Campus Police" and their accommodation office will let you know what the rules are relating to reporting unsociable behaviour.

- Meet the students and parents when they book in and make sure they book into an immaculate property – many times they will return the favour and leave it that way; but if parents have to clean before they say adieu to their children, you will always get it back in the same tired state.

- You will need to improve and decorate more often: allow for the costs in your projections.

- Doing your own gardening is a good way of keeping an eye on how things are going.

- Do three inspections per year – put them in the contract.

- Insist that students host visits by next year's potential tenants.

- Make sure deposits are dealt with correctly, as it's the only legal way you can deduct money if you need to at the end of the tenancy.

- Have a thorough inventory, with detailed pictures.

- Allow for replacing some items every year.

- Consider soundproofing party walls where families live next door (this may also be required of you by the local authority).

Consider what students want:

- A good, high speed internet connection. Broadband is essential and it's best if the landlord provides and pays for it.

- A desk in each room.

- Consider a "bills included" contract. Parents (who are also guarantors) and students prefer this.

- The University's Accommodation Office will provide a checklist of items to be provided in each room.

Similarly, think about what professionals want if renting to them. For example:

- In-room cooking and washing facilities, if possible.

- More showers, preferably ensuite.

It is worth seeking guidance especially if you are inexperienced, as you don't know what you don't know. Did you know for example that you should check the 'right to rent' of foreign students? However, ARLA (the Association of Residential Letting Agents) has agreed with the Home Office a template letter that can be used by agents to get around the Right to Rent issues with regard to foreign students.

What Could Go Wrong?

Every strategy in property carries its own set of risks. In addition to the more expected factors such as health and safety and tenant problems, here are some additional potential risks:

- **Oversupply:** I was surprised to find this being discussed as an issue by some HMO landlords when I recently attended a property networking event in south London, although it was not too clear whether this was partly down to some landlords trying to push up rents too high.

- **Build-to-rent developers moving into the area:** The problem of oversupply can be hugely aggravated by build-to-rent developers moving into the area and this has caused problems for HMO landlords in some areas, with some university towns particularly targeted. Know your area and keep abreast of any property news that could affect your business, and be prepared to take what action you can to ensure your HMO continues to be profitable.

- **Not knowing the rules:** The rules and regulations surrounding HMOs are complex and you must be prepared to put in the time and work to learn about them and keep up to date. The information given in this chapter will help you to make a start, but it is important to keep in touch with changes locally and nationally. Look at the references below, keep current through relevant newsletters and groups, and stay in touch with news from the local council.

Further Reading, Resources and References

Residential Landlords Association (RLA) information on the definition of HMOs: https://www.rla.org.uk/landlord/guides/housing_act/docs/all/what_is_an_hmo.shtml

Jim Haliburton, who calls himself the HMO Daddy, teaches and has written several books on HMOs. See https://www.hmodaddy.com/

Book: *Complete HMO Property Success*, Nick Fox (Jan 2016)

For national guidance on HMOs: https://www.gov.uk/private-renting/houses-in-multiple-occupation

To find your local council: https://www.gov.uk/find-local-council

For more on building regulations and planning: https://www.planningportal.co.uk

How does this strategy appeal to you?

Rate this strategy, on a scale from 0 - 10, for the following factors:

0 . 1 . 2 . 3 . 4 . 5 . 6 . 7 . 8 . 9 . 10 **Time**

0 . 1 . 2 . 3 . 4 . 5 . 6 . 7 . 8 . 9 . 10 **Money**

0 . 1 . 2 . 3 . 4 . 5 . 6 . 7 . 8 . 9 . 10 **Risk**

0 . 1 . 2 . 3 . 4 . 5 . 6 . 7 . 8 . 9 . 10 **Appeal**

0 . 1 . 2 . 3 . 4 . 5 . 6 . 7 . 8 . 9 . 10 **Knowledge**

0 . 1 . 2 . 3 . 4 . 5 . 6 . 7 . 8 . 9 . 10 **Aptitude**

0 . 1 . 2 . 3 . 4 . 5 . 6 . 7 . 8 . 9 . 10 **Tax**

CHAPTER 6

SHORT-TERM LETS –
Serviced Accommodation, Holiday Lets, Airbnb

"The obstacle is the way"

Ancient saying

Introduction

The short-term let industry has been revolutionised by Airbnb and similar platforms that allow people to offer and book short stays easily online or via an app, either in people's homes or in privately-owned serviced accommodation.

The pressures exerted by government on the private rented sector have left many investors in urgent need of increasing returns, which is at least partly responsible for the phenomenal success of serviced accommodation and Airbnb in recent years.

The income from short-term lets is even more enhanced than the income from HMOs when compared to that from vanilla buy-to-let. You could say they are like the Three Billy Goats Gruff, each bigger than the last!

The graph below shows the monthly rent achievable in each case including a short-term let (STL).

The gross income in this example for a single let is £1,000 per month, for an HMO £2,000 and for a short-term let £3,000 (based on rates in my local area of an equivalent property, being £100 per night). The work of managing grows more intensive from BTL to HMO to STL and the viability becomes more critically dependent on location.

Figure 2: Graph of Gross Monthly Income Achievable by Type of Let

While you can expect gross rents for short-term lets to be up to three times higher than buy-to-let, and more than HMOs too, in practice there are bound to be void periods between bookings, and the actual income may largely depend on demand. In turn, demand will be affected not only by location, but the effectiveness of your marketing, as well as the ratings and reviews that the property receives.

There are niches within short lets. As well as tourists and holidaymakers, demand for short-term lets can come from various groups including business visitors or corporate guests, contract workers, labourers, and homeowners looking for temporary accommodation while in the process of relocating.

It is good to get an idea of the type of visitors that the location is likely to attract, so you can tailor your marketing efforts towards that group. The target market may also affect where you buy, how you set the place up, and where you advertise.

Short-term lets allow for flexibility in pricing. You can adjust prices to meet higher levels of demand, for example in peak season, or around the time of significant local events. By adjusting your prices appropriately, you can achieve a higher potential income over the course of the year.

There is much more to the business of short-term lets than just the potential for enhanced income. It is more akin to the leisure and hotel industry than simple buy-to-let; and it is advisable to tread carefully when you first enter this potentially lucrative yet challenging market. Remember the 80/20 principle – or 90/10!

For some buy-to-let landlords, a six-month rental may still be the right choice, as it provides a steady income without the need to find a series of tenants and deal with all the headaches and extra admin that short-term lets can entail. If you give it a try, be prepared to do the work. Setting a place up and getting the hang of the marketing for the first time is bound to be especially challenging, but once your systems are in place and you have established a satisfactory level of demand, things should get easier.

The strategy of short-term lets can be combined with other strategies, for example some operators take on rent-to-rent properties to offer as short-term lets. Others develop whole blocks of serviced apartments, sometimes complete with reception areas. Or you may turn your buy-to-let or HMO into an Airbnb or holiday let.

A Word on Holiday Lets and Other Types of Short-Term Let

Holiday lets can appear almost overlooked in this new age of **Airbnb, Booking.com**, **serviced accommodation** /or **apartments**. There is still a place for holiday lets and some like to make this distinction, but they are often considered as a form or variant of short-term lets.

I found when researching this chapter that different people use different terminology and the lack of standardisation can cause some confusion. Some people use **serviced accommodation** to cover all varieties of residential **short-term lets**. Others, including myself, may switch between terms! **Short let properties** is another variant that is sometimes used.

Some people have strong views, for example insisting, "I do holiday lets, that's different", while expressing distaste for "Airbnb lets". Holiday lets and serviced accommodation (including serviced apartments) are arguably the same thing normally, while Airbnb (along with Booking.com and others) is not a type of let but a web-based platform that allows people to offer and book any type of short-term lets.

Booking.com advertises hotel rooms alongside private lets. Note however, that hotels are normally purpose built and operate under a different planning Use Class, whereas the recent phenomenon of short-term lets with which this chapter is mainly concerned tend to be operated from residential properties and this is a significant difference.

Traditional holiday lets were normally located, even clustered, in seaside or tourist areas, or often in rural areas of outstanding natural beauty, again attracting mainly holidaymakers.

The new era of serviced accommodation has become more and more popular in built-up residential areas and sometimes attracts bad press, as neighbours can be disturbed by occasional rowdy guests.

Furthermore, while traditional holiday lets are normally well defined with adherence to all the rules, including mortgage type and insurance, some who operate from ordinary residential premises (and particularly in the case of flats) may not have all the correct measures in place, which can also give the industry a bad name. We will look at these issues later in the chapter.

Serviced Accommodation or Apartments

Self-contained serviced apartments can be distinguished from serviced accommodation offered on a room-only basis (as opposed to a whole property or self-contained apartment) which may even be in a host's own home.

Serviced apartments can be further defined as one or other of the following:

- **Serviced Apartments** – Self-contained apartments normally within a residential building. There may or may not be staff on site. Guests often have access to a 24-hour helpline.

- **Aparthotels** – serviced apartments within a dedicated building, offering hotel-like services with a 24-hour reception. These may also offer additional facilities like a communal lounge or an on-site gym. Some operators call their apartments '*suites*' within an aparthotel.

- **Corporate Housing** – a furnished apartment or house made available for rent or lease on a temporary basis, often 30 days or more. The corporate travel world has long seen the advantage of this kind of accommodation for executives on longer business trips or during relocations, as they allow the traveller a more 'normal' way of life than hotels, with the chance to cook, relax and plan their time away from hotel operating hours.

Airbnb and Other Platforms

Airbnb and other similar websites have become widely known and popular platforms to advertise or book your serviced apartments, rooms or holiday lets.

Over 4 million people have stayed in an Airbnb in London since it launched in 2008. It took six years for the room-rental startup to reach 1 million guest arrivals, but just over two years to hit 4 million.

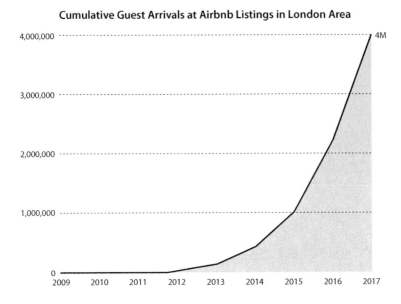

Figure 3: Source: uk.businessinsider.com reporting on Airbnb statistics

In the summer of 2010, around 47,000 people worldwide stayed at properties advertised on Airbnb; by the summer of 2015 the number had rocketed to almost 17 million. Conceived as a simple means of letting out a spare room, the site has morphed into something much larger.

Airbnb offers free listings to property owners and lets travellers browse the listings for free too. The platform makes its money when bookings are made, charging a 10% commission to hosts and 3% of the booking amount to travellers upon making their booking.

Airbnb is not the only site offering such a service and many landlords and property owners list their properties on several similar sites (fees vary) including:

- Airbnb

- Booking.com

- Expedia

- LateRooms.com

- HomeAway.co.uk

- TripAdvisor

It is worth having a look at these other platforms to see which may suit your property.

High Street Agents

Alternatively, some high street agents will also market and deal with short-term lets, particularly in areas where the demand for this type of accommodation is high such as in big cities.

Letting agents who deal with short-term lets, mostly ranging from a few weeks to six months (the maximum length for a short let), will often charge around double the long-term letting fee.

More Ways to Market Your Short Stay Property

Don't forget the power of social media of course, as well as offline, and having your own website:

- Social Media: Facebook, Twitter, Pinterest, Linkedin

- Email marketing

- Offline marketing

- Your website

Channel Managers

Channel Managers help you with updating your bookings calendar across the various booking sites and more. Take a look at:

- www.guesty.com

- www.freetobook.com

- www.eviivo.com

Location: Research the Demand and Restrictions

Research the demand in your area or buy where there is demand. Look around at what other serviced accommodation may be available in the area, what hotels there are and what ratings they tend to be at. What tourist attractions are there in your area, if any? Or, what business might bring people to the area – specifically contractors? One person I know specialises in renting houses on short-term lets to building contractors in Milton Keynes, where there is a demand for that type of accommodation from that type of guest for periods of 3-4 months at a time.

Be very clear about your market and the type of guests you are looking to get. There's no point having high-end fittings if you are not going for a high-end market. Make sure the property works as a single let, so it could work if you need to revert back to single lets.

The short-term lets model has a few different angles. One operator I spoke to has mainly corporate guests from overseas companies who find short-term lets cheaper than their contractors staying in a hotel. They also save money on food costs as they are more likely to eat in than go out.

Of course, there will be more demand in city centres as a rule, especially big cities like London. However, remember that planning restrictions in London limit the nights you can do short-term lets to 90 per year.

Planning and Use Class

The English planning system assigns a 'Use Class' to sites, for example a shop falls under A1 Use Class, most offices are B1 and a restaurant is A3. (The Scottish planning system is different and Wales has some variations too.)

The Use Class for Planning purposes of a normal residential property or buy-to-let is C3; for an HMO (up to 6 people) it is C4; and for hotels C1.

There is currently no specific Use Class for short-term lets / serviced accommodation, so it appears there is no definitive answer as to whether serviced accommodation can be operated under Use Class C3 as a normal residential property. It is instead open to interpretation according to the local council, and I found disagreement on the matter among other commentators.

I am not a planning expert, I am just reporting the overall impression I get from the research I have done and the people I have spoken to. Given that many people are implementing the strategy and operating short-term lets from residential properties in many areas of the country without any change of use class, it seems that many councils are not dictating that planning permission is required for change of use. One interpretation is that short-term lets are allowed under 'permitted development rights', and others say that no change of use requirement exists.

Up until a few years ago, there was no separate Use Class for HMOs but one was created as they grew in popularity. It is likewise possible, in future, that a separate Use Class will be created for residential short-term lets. It is important meanwhile to contact your local council to ask their opinion on what you can or cannot do if you wish to start this form of letting.

Some areas, notably the whole of London, apply Article 4 planning restrictions to short-term lets (as are applied to HMOs in some areas), and do not allow properties to be rented out on a short-term basis for more than 90 days per year. Airbnb now restricts the marketing of properties in London to a maximum of 90 days per year accordingly. Always seek advice for your area.

Bear in mind that if you are required to change to C1 Use Class, business rates will be payable instead of council tax.

Serviced Accommodation From the Guests' Point of View

There are a variety of reasons why guests might enjoy a stay at your short-let property instead of choosing to stay at a hotel. It partly depends of course on the set up and location – whether it is a self-contained apartment or a room which may be in the host's own home.

For travellers who choose to stay as a guest in someone's home, reasons may include:

- It is often cheaper than staying in a hotel (this applies to room lets not in a host's home too);

- They may want an experience of what life is like for the locals;

- The property may be ideally situated for their purposes;

- They may welcome the knowledge of the area that the hosts may be able to share;

- They may feel safer or cosier in somebody's home than in a hotel.

Serviced apartments are fast becoming a popular choice for leisure and business travellers in major cities. The benefits of serviced apartments for guests include:

- **Space:** On average, serviced apartments offer 30% more space than a standard hotel equivalent.

- **Value for money:** The prices for serviced apartments are typically 20% less than hotel rates for the same standard. Some providers allow for bookings to be cheaper when only required for Monday - Friday, for example for guests who are staying for work purposes.

- **Home from home:** Serviced apartments offer a home-from-home experience that you don't get from staying in a hotel room, offering comfort, space – often with a separate living room, and flexibility.

- **Cooking and washing facilities:** Having your own kitchen is convenient and cost-effective, so you can cook in the apartment instead of having to eat out as you would do staying in a hotel. Kitchens often come complete with a washer/dryer as well as cooker, fridge-freezer and even a dishwasher.

- **Privacy and security:** Guests enjoy the greater privacy of serviced apartments over hotels and may feel safer in a self-contained private environment. Housekeeping services are often weekly, which many prefer over having cleaners coming in daily or even more often, as they do in hotels.

- **Additional services:** Some apartments offer the chance to order bespoke services such as stocking the kitchen cupboards with the guest's favourite treats.

Setting Up and Running Serviced Accommodation

Setting up and running your serviced accommodation business will take time, money and effort.

As already touched upon in the previous section about what guests expect, you will have to maintain **standards** that are comparable to a hotel while offering additional facilities too. Always consider **health and safety** in everything, particularly in the kitchen area and concerning gas, electrical items and fire safety.

Make sure your apartment is **well decorated** and has **quality furnishings**, paying particular attention to the bed and the **kitchen appliances**, as well as providing a good TV, wifi and other home comforts.

An apartment will need to be **fully furnished**, down to cutlery and crockery and everything you would normally expect to find in a well-equipped kitchen.

Remember that you will also need to provide **clean linen and towels**. Some operators hire these and use a service that will clean and replace as required. You can find such services online for most big towns and cities.

Unless you are willing to do the cleaning yourself, you will need **a reliable cleaner** and their role will be very important – especially if you want them to also keep an eye on the place for you and report on the condition after each guest's stay. You may even ask the cleaner to meet and greet guests if they can be relied on to portray the right image.

It is a good idea to provide **a manual for the cleaner**, detailing what jobs they should do and what they should report back to you. You could also get them to go around checking that everything is in working order, including lights, appliances, shower and so on. Give clear instructions and provide them with a checklist.

You will also need **tradesmen** who can help with maintenance when required, as with any property; and bear in mind that any delays in fixing things could mean that the property is unlettable while waiting for things to be fixed that it would be unacceptable to have not working, such as the shower.

Create a **guest manual** and include everything they need to know about how to work the washing machine, cooker, shower, TV, wifi and so on. Also include emergency procedures such as fire exit and who to call in an emergency. Give information about local transport, amenities and things to do.

Photographs: If you list on Airbnb, they will send someone to do professional photos for you (if they have someone available in the area). Dress the property to look its best for the photos but make sure the reality lives up to the photos too!

Taking payments: Most of the online platforms such as Airbnb will arrange to take payments on your behalf – and take their commission automatically. If you take bookings through your own website or other means of independent advertising, you will need to set up ways of taking payments at the time of booking. Consider taking payments via www.paypal.com, www.worldpay.com or www.stripe.com.

Keys and access: Think about whether you want to meet and greet guests or get someone to do this for you, or whether to enable access via a key box or other electronic access code. Some people have a key safe box at the property: most models allow you to program multiple user codes, making it easy to create and delete unique codes for your guests. Alternatively, smart locks replace the code-based method with an electronic system that unlocks when it receives a wireless signal from an authorized smartphone, and do away with the need for keys.

Checks after guests: You will need to check on the property after guests to ensure all is well and there are no breakages. If there are any problems, you may have to take steps to withhold monies from any security deposit taken. If booking through platforms such as Airbnb, they can offer help and advice on this.

Managing your bookings: If you are taking bookings across multiple platforms, it can be hard to keep track. You can get software that helps with the management and marketing of your properties, such as the channel managers mentioned earlier including www.guesty.com which offers a range of features.

Mortgages for Short-Term and Holiday Lets

You will require a suitable mortgage that allows for the use of the property for short-term lets. You may wish to ask permission from a current lender, but it is unlikely to be granted in most cases.

Of the big high street lenders, only Nationwide and Santander allow a form of Airbnb-type letting of an entire primary property – albeit with an additional charge. A few other lenders permit this on second homes.

Market Harborough Building Society (MHBS) has a mortgage designed especially for landlords using Airbnb and similar sites.

MHBS has a holiday let range for landlords as well as a residential mortgage through which borrowers can let their main residence for up to 24 weeks a year. The catch with both products is that the rates are high. The holiday-let rate is currently 4.49%, at a maximum 70% loan-to-value. A similar, standard buy-to-let deal can cost about 2.3%, with a £2,000 arrangement fee.

Several other building societies offer flexibility by allowing either holiday or short-term lets, including Leeds Building Society, Bath, Cumberland, Furness, and Harpenden.

However, they do not all permit lettings via sites such as Airbnb. For example, Leeds says its mortgages support permanent holiday lets and not intermittent short-term letting, such as occasional Airbnb lets.

As lenders become more aware of the popularity among landlords of short-term lets via sites such as Airbnb, further products are starting to be made available. Specialist lender Together recently introduced a holiday let product that allows for marketing on Airbnb.

Insurance

You must arrange for the property to be adequately insured for short lets. An ordinary policy is unlikely to provide sufficient cover for the additional risks. In addition to specialist buildings and contents cover, liability insurance – for injury or damage – and loss of income in the event of a fire or a burst pipe, for example, are recommended.

Tax Treatment of Short-Term Lets

Short-term lets are treated differently for tax purposes by HMRC as Furnished Holiday Lets and, significantly, such income is exempt from the removal of mortgage interest relief that buy-to-let has suffered.

VAT

If your total income from short lets is over the threshold for VAT (currently £83,000), you will need to register for VAT.

What Could Possibly Go Wrong?

The potentially high income of short-term lets may be hard to resist, but the high rates compensate for the additional effort and risk involved in renting out properties short-term.

Two big issues that landlords face with short lets are void periods and wear and tear. Short lets bring flexibility but also uncertainty, and some voids are to be expected with short-term lets.

You will need to cover costs in a short let that would normally be paid by a long-term tenant, such as utility bills, internet, TV licence and council tax. The property will also need to be fully furnished and well equipped, all of which means additional expense that needs to be taken into account.

Less welcome guests may include groups wanting to hire a party venue, which most landlords will be keen to avoid for obvious reasons. The noise and disruption such 'guests' can cause is what gives short-term lets a bad name in some quarters. Some owners have a policy of not taking bookings for less than three nights which can help to avoid the property being used as a party venue. Some will also not take bookings from same sex parties under the age of 25.

Leasehold properties

Leasehold properties, mainly flats, may have a restriction on the lease that prevents the property being used for short-term lets and this needs to be checked before you can even consider short-term lets for a flat. The freeholder may restrict short lets in the building either through covenants in the lease, or by demanding additional fees, as they are often not keen due to the potential for noise and disruption for other residents.

Risks and Warnings

I spoke with Giles Peaker, litigation solicitor at Anthony Gold Solicitors, who recently dealt with a case where a landlord was being sued after an Airbnb guest fell from the balcony of his flat, where he had no permission or suitable insurance in place to sub-let on a short-term basis.

Vanessa Warwick of Property Tribes commented: *"In Greater London there is a specific planning restriction which says property can only be used for short-term lets for up to 90 days per year. Above that and it's in breach of the planning rules – you would have to have full-blown planning permission to do it and if you haven't got that, potentially you can be facing prosecution by the local authority. I know some local councils – certainly in central London – are looking very closely at this and they are looking closely at Airbnb use and the ways in which properties are being advertised on it."*

Recent research by the National Landlords Association showed that many properties are being made available all year round for Airbnb-style lettings, even in areas where restrictions are imposed.

In a video interview with Giles Peaker, Vanessa said: *"Some people are also saying they will advertise empty rooms in HMOs on Airbnb, but this seems wrong."* He agreed, saying, *"It could put women in danger for example; you have strangers coming into a house of co-habitants and that makes them vulnerable."* Both agree that letting rooms on a short-term let basis within an HMO set-up is not a good idea and that the two should not be mixed.

Vanessa linked to an article stating that Liverpool council are also looking to take action against short-term lets, with the headline: *"The Echo revealed 'party let' properties are making residents' lives hell."*

Adequate insurance to cover you against damage, accidents, liability and loss of earnings is essential. Take out a policy that is designed specifically for your property.

Keep accurate accounts of income and expenditure for tax purposes and declare all earnings from your property when filing your annual return to HMRC.

Make sure your property complies with health and safety regulations before you put it on the market.

The Association of Serviced Apartment Providers (ASAP) promotes professional standards; see the website at www.theasap.org.uk.

In conclusion, landlords aspiring to do well with short-term lets need to stick to certain guidelines. Do further reading and research. Consider getting some training or expert advice; make sure you play by the rules with regard to planning as well as mortgages; and take out specialist insurance.

Further Reading, Resources and References

E-book: *Serviced Apartments, An A – Z*, Carole Cooney (Nov 2016)

Book: *The Serviced Accommodation Success Manual*, Paul Smith (2017)

www.airbnb.co

http://uk.businessinsider.com/airbnb-growth-in-london-number-of-guests-surpass-4-million-2017-1

www.gov.uk/apply-for-business-rate-relief/small-business-rate-relief

http://theasap.org.uk/non-members-consumers/about-serviced-apartments/what-is-a-serviced-apartment/

https://www.mortgagestrategy.co.uk/cover-feature-getaway-vehicles/

https://www.gov.uk/government/publications/furnished-holiday-lettings-hs253-self-assessment-helpsheet/hs253-furnished-holiday-lettings-2015

https://www.propertytribes.com/air-b-n-b-serviced-accommodation-reality-t-127628787.html

http://www.thesapodcast.com/03-planning-use-class/

People recommended for more advice on short-term lets:

Jason Living teaches serviced accommodation (find via Facebook).

Jane Skynner – holiday lets and interior design (find via Facebook).

Vanessa Warwick of www.propertytribes.com, holiday lets.

Giles Peaker, solicitor, Anthony Gold Solicitors; property solicitor who acts in dispute cases.

How does this strategy appeal to you?

Rate this strategy, on a scale from 0 - 10, for the following factors:

0 . 1 . 2 . 3 . 4 . 5 . 6 . 7 . 8 . 9 . 10   **Time**

0 . 1 . 2 . 3 . 4 . 5 . 6 . 7 . 8 . 9 . 10   **Money**

0 . 1 . 2 . 3 . 4 . 5 . 6 . 7 . 8 . 9 . 10   **Risk**

0 . 1 . 2 . 3 . 4 . 5 . 6 . 7 . 8 . 9 . 10   **Appeal**

0 . 1 . 2 . 3 . 4 . 5 . 6 . 7 . 8 . 9 . 10   **Knowledge**

0 . 1 . 2 . 3 . 4 . 5 . 6 . 7 . 8 . 9 . 10   **Aptitude**

0 . 1 . 2 . 3 . 4 . 5 . 6 . 7 . 8 . 9 . 10   **Tax**

CHAPTER 7

ESTATE AGENTS –
SALES AND LETTINGS

*"Customer service is not a department,
it's everyone's job."*

Anonymous

So, You Want to Be an Estate Agent?

In planning this chapter, it struck me that there are various ways to go about becoming an estate agent (*the term estate agent being used to refer also to the lettings side in a wider sense*), and how you approach the matter may depend on your background, experience and mindset. I suppose this is true in any field, but estate agency provides a stark illustration.

When you want to get ahead and generate income, how do you go about it? Do you:

- Get formal qualifications, maybe even a degree?

- Buy a book or course material that could help you; or attend a short course?

- Think in terms of working for somebody else?

- Perhaps become a franchisee?

- Or do you start up your own business?

The truth is, any of these approaches can work and it all depends on you, your experience, confidence and mindset. You might start in one way, then later swap to another approach.

If you are unsure whether estate agency is for you, you could consider working part-time in a local estate agents' office, to give it a try.

You do not usually need to have previous experience in estate agency when you start out, but in order to join the National Association of Estate Agents (NAEA) you have to be working in the sector, to have professional indemnity insurance and to join the Property Ombudsman scheme. (www.tpos.co.uk). In practice, this makes it difficult to start out on your own without some qualifications.

As the law stands today, there is no UK-wide statutory regulation of managing agents (although rules vary for Scotland, Wales and Northern Ireland, where housing policy is devolved) but there are increasing calls for more regulation to drive up standards, from professional bodies such as the NAEA as well as ARLA (The Association of Residential Property Agents), the National Landlords Association (NLA) and Residential Landlords Association (RLA). Many agents already submit to voluntary regulation and I would strongly suggest to landlords to look out for what professional bodies agents belong to.

In this chapter, in addition to looking at agents from a landlord's point of view, we will look at the industry specific qualifications you could get to become an estate agent and at the possibility of becoming a franchisee or starting your own estate and/or letting agency business.

If you're young and inexperienced, a job working for an established estate agency could be a great way to start your property journey. While a degree level education is certainly not necessary, a good education will hopefully always stand you in good stead and can help in a competitive jobs market.

If you are looking for a job in this field, starting salaries for estate agents are in the region of £12,000 to £20,000 for trainees, rising to £25,000 to £60,000 plus commission, with experience, or even more in London.

If you are looking to set up your own business, you will likely be hoping to generate a greater income from the business, but you also take on the risk as well as the set-up costs and measures. This will be discussed in the sections on **Becoming a Franchisee** and **A Quick Start to Your Own Business.**

Estate agents' commissions on sales can range from fixed fees as low as the £595 charged by online agents www.zoom995.co.uk who we often use, up to 1% (plus VAT if applicable) of the sale price, which can easily run into thousands. For example, a fairly average priced property at £250,000 would produce a commission of £2,500 from a fee of 1%.

Estate agents often have links with financial advisors, solicitors and surveyors additionally, and get paid commission when their clients use these services.

On the lettings side, fees for property management also vary depending on the service provided (as discussed more fully later) but can be as much as 10% or even more of the monthly rent, in addition to various set-up fees such as tenant find and inventories. So, on a rent for example of £1,200 per month, you could easily be earning £120 per month for each property, or £1,440 per year. With just 20 properties under management, this could give you an ongoing income approaching £30,000 a year, before taking into account other charges.

There are various types of estate agency and they tend to specialise, although many businesses include both a sales and lettings side:

- Residential sales;

- Residential lettings;

- Commercial sales;

- Commercial lettings;

- Rural estate agents (this often includes land and rural businesses including farms).

Whether working for yourself or others, it is vital to develop a good knowledge of the local property market in the area of specialisation you want to work in, as well as good customer service skills.

Specific Qualifications for Estate and Letting Agents

Whilst industry specific qualifications may not be required to start with, they are recommended for your ongoing professional development, as they will help your knowledge and understanding of the work involved, as well as strengthening your credentials.

NAEA Propertymark (see www.naea.co.uk) is the UK's leading professional body for estate agency. They offer a range of short courses for those working in England, Wales and Northern Ireland. When I was considering a franchise with EweMove, I decided to study for the Propertymark Qualifications. At the time, they came under the NFOPP (National Federation of Property Professionals Awarding Body).

The qualifications I got were the Level 3 Award in Residential Letting & Property Management (QCF) and Level 3 Award in The Sale of Residential Property (QCF), which formed the basis of the criteria required to join ARLA (the Association of Residential Letting Agents), the UK's largest professional body for letting agents, and the NAEA (National Association of Estate Agents).

Some jobs may require qualification and membership of the Royal Institution of Chartered Surveyors (RICS). To find more information on these qualifications, visit the NAEA Propertymark website.

The Residential Letting & Property Management programme that I did consisted of four units broadly:

- Health and Safety, Security and General Law

- Legal Aspects of Letting and Management

- Residential Property Letting Practice

- Residential Property Management Practice

The Sale of Residential Property programme consisted of four units too, some very similar:

- Health and Safety, Security and General Law

- Law Relating to Residential Property Sales

- Practice Relating to Residential Property Sales

- Property Appraisal and Basic Building Construction/Defects

The RLA (Residential Landlords' Association) also run various courses including a short course called the **Agents Guide to Lettings**:

> *"This course is ideal for Letting Agents new to the sector along with those with vast experience. It serves as both an introduction to the Private Rented Sector and a refresher. For those of you who require an overview of the lettings process to understand your obligations from start to finish this course will give you an overview from finding a tenant to ending the tenancy. For agents who already have a good understanding of the lettings process this course will serve as a useful refresher and enable you to identify the many industry updates of late."*

Roles and Responsibilities

Estate agency is very varied and interesting work that requires good organisational skills. You will also need skills such as:

- Negotiating with clients, persuading them to use your services and achieving success for them;

- Excellent communication skills, to gain trust and to reassure clients, as well as liaising with other professionals;

- IT skills.

The roles of an estate agent include the need to:

- Visit and talk to sellers about the property and advise them of your estimation of value;

- Gather information about a property, including measuring up and taking photographs;

- Market properties effectively, testing and measuring the effectiveness of the marketing;

- Represent sellers in negotiations with buyers;

- Monitor ongoing sales to ensure they stay on track, including liaising with mortgage brokers, solicitors, surveyors and others.

In addition, for lettings, you will need to:

- Vet prospective tenants by checking references and carrying out credit checks;

- Undertake or arrange inventories, to carefully record the property condition prior to commencement of a tenancy;

- Draw up tenancy agreements;

- Organise collection of rent payments and deposits; and hand on rent less commission to landlords;

- Ensure properties meet all legal requirements including health and safety and any additional regulations that may apply.

Taking on a Franchise

Becoming a franchisee is one way to start out with all the support you need and can give you a great business if you work at it and are right for the job. All franchise companies will require you to give part of your profits to the franchisor as part of your ongoing agreement with them, while they should offer ongoing benefits in return such as tapping into their systems and support from head office, as well as ongoing professional training and opportunities to get together with other franchisees for support.

You can become a EweMove franchisee for as little as £1,500 + VAT but prices vary depending on the area, your experience and other factors. Some franchises cost considerably more and require you to get high street premises which can be expensive, but EweMove do not. Other well-known franchises include Belvoir Lettings, Your Move, Northwood and others. More information about franchises can be found via the British Franchise Association (BFA). Since it can be expensive to be a member, not all franchises necessarily belong, including ones that are quite newly established, although they can represent a good opportunity to get in early at lower cost.

Many years ago, before I got established in property, I had a fascination with the idea of getting a franchise and considered a range of opportunities. There are magazines on the subject of franchising and an annual national show you can attend if interested. It is an exciting area to look into but remember, franchises all cost money to join and your success is never guaranteed! Also, you will not have as much autonomy as if you started your own business.

I became a franchisee for five years (from 2004 to 2009) of a company that focused on marketing for properties to buy below market value, A Quick Sale Ltd (AQS). After the market crash of 2008 and changes in the lending market, many of us left the company and a couple of the directors broke away to start focusing on managing the big portfolios they had accumulated.

Glenn Ackroyd and **David Laycock** built great systems for property management, and soon started to attract others who asked them to manage their portfolios as well, so they set up a company to manage properties for themselves and others, originally named The National Property Group (NPG).

They specialised in rent-to-buy initially – a great way to get tenants to treat property like their own home, because it soon would be. It also gave landlords a clear exit. It can work very well – I still have several of these that are managed by the company which Glenn and David set up. The company later became another franchise and changed its name to **EweMove.com**.

In fact, as EweMove evolved into a franchise-based company, it attracted many people previously from AQS to become franchisees. As I missed working with a group of people (rather than being drawn by the income), I went along with a view to signing up – although later decided not to, due to other priorities.

If you are very ambitious, you could aim to set up a franchise and later sell the business, like Glenn Ackroyd and David Laycock of EweMove did! I interviewed Glenn Ackroyd for this book and you can see his replies in Appendix III.

A Quick Start To Your Own Business

If you are very entrepreneurial, you could set up your own agency or chain, like **John Paul** of **Castle Estates** did. John Paul is also well-known in property circles and has recently published a book, *From Stress to Success; How to Build a Successful Business that Operates Without You*. That is certainly on my reading list! John is known for being a fervent believer in the power of systemising your business.

A big question for agents will always be whether to set up with a physical presence on the high street, or work from home. Alternatively, you could of course have an office in a cheaper part of town. The cost of renting high street premises can run into thousands and in many areas is unlikely to be viable for a startup, if that is your main source of income. Luckily, it is possible to run your business from home and many people do. In this internet age and with the advent of online agents, I believe that people are generally more open to dealing with agents that are not on the high street.

If you want to go it alone but are looking for a good source of information and support, Southcourt Property (www.southcourtproperty.co.uk) have been going for over 20 years, since 1997, with their offering of "the UK's number one new agency business package". I got their pack many years ago, in 2003, when I was first thinking of managing properties for others, so I was interested to see they are still going strong. I found the package very good and certainly good value. When I got their package in 2003, it was for lettings only, but the package now includes the sales side of estate agency too.

Their current (2018) prices range from £275-£525 (on *special offer*) with the higher price levels including support with setting up a website and other marketing tools. They do not require you to pay them any commission and they offer ongoing support. No previous business experience or qualifications are required. The package offers a comprehensive plan for setting up your business and even includes template letters and documents. This is a very practical approach for those that want to *just do it*.

Letting Agents, a Landlord's Perspective

Many readers of this book will be landlords and investors who may be more likely to use the services of letting and estate agents than to be one, and therefore this section takes a look at letting agents from the landlord/client's perspective.

Agents vary from small, local independents to national chains and anything in between. They can be online, offline or a hybrid. The services they offer can vary from acting as little more than gateways, to advertising your property on portals such as Rightmove and others to full property management, and they can also act as estate agents or have that covered within the same business.

Some agents like to get into heated debates, fiercely defending their service options compared to others, but it's good for consumers to have choices. Personally, I've used every type of service from none (ie complete self-management) to full management by agents and can see advantages in all.

Obviously, cost is a factor and generally the less input from agents, the lower the cost, but remember there can be hidden costs in making mistakes if you try to do things yourself: see my example later of the agent who got me £20,000 more for the sale of my property than I might have accepted in an unfamiliar area. Mistakes can be not only costly but get you into trouble too, such as not drawing up a tenancy agreement correctly or following proper health and safety procedures.

I have used www.upad.co.uk which is one of the lowest cost ways to get your property listed on Rightmove and other portals. Prices start from £120 and include tenant referencing for which the tenant pays. (They also offer more premium service levels.) Upad take initial calls and enquiries which they pass on to the landlord and then it's up to you to get back to enquirers. You must organise your own viewings. I found it best to arrange for all viewers to come to the property on one day, especially for non-local properties. You do have to be a bit brave to do this, I found!

Locally, we now use the Tenant Find Only service of an online estate agent www.zoom995.co.uk and we also use them when selling. For sales, they charge just £595 inc VAT if paid upfront or £995 at completion (hence the name zoom995). Their fee for tenant find only is just £295 and they will do viewings and arrange an inventory (for an extra cost) and an EPC if required. We find them very helpful and they have good contacts with local tradesmen too. They also offer a fully managed service for £49.50 inc VAT per month. They are 'an online agent' but can – depending on location – arrange to do viewings. They are prepared to travel to any part of the UK and have links with other agents too.

Years ago, we used to simply place a classified ad in the local paper when we had a property available to let. That was cheap! The local council came across one of our adverts and contacted us about taking benefit tenants via their 'tenants' deposit scheme'. At the time we could get higher rents from this, so we started letting to benefit tenants through the council and did not have to worry about advertising for years. There was certainly no shortage of benefit tenants who wanted housing.

We also worked with a local housing charity that sought accommodation for their clients. However, when the system for calculating rental allowances changed to LHA (the local housing allowance), rents no longer kept pace with what you could get renting to working people, which is why we stopped. With the S24 tax changes, like other landlords we had to maximise our rents.

I also have a group of properties that I bought below market value non-locally (using sourcers), specifically for rent-to-buy, when I developed a great enthusiasm for the strategy a few years ago, up until I hit my target of owning 100 properties. It may seem almost childish but I was dead set on reaching that target number of properties, although Dave had had enough of more properties to manage – so I was buying these to hand over directly for full management to EweMove, who in their early days focused on the rather specialised strategy of rent-to-buy, which is when tenants sign up to rent now and buy later, under an option agreement set up in addition to the usual AST (assured shorthold tenancy agreement).

While the rent-to-buy scheme was an added motivation for me to use EweMove, the full management service has been a blessing in saving me the hassle of managing those properties from afar.

Chart of Letting Agents' Services

It is helpful to consider the various aspects of property management that might be on offer under various levels of service in table form, as below. The exact parameters will vary from one agent to another, so always check. Could you see yourself doing all these things as a self-managing landlord, or would you rather use an agent? Or indeed, become an agent offering such services?

- **Listing and tenant-find only**: as discussed above, agents may charge from £120 for listing-only. We pay £295 + VAT for tenant-find but fees for this can be up to 1-1.5 months' rent.

- **Rent collection service:** may be around 5%-7%. This service does not include dealing with maintenance, which the landlord would organise themselves.

- **Full management:** may be anything from around 8%-10% or more.

- **Extras:** Some agents will include things that others charge as extras, for example drawing up the AST (assured shorthold tenancy agreement).

Services	Listing Services	Tenant-Find Only	Rent Collection	Full Management
Market appraisal with comparables guide		✓	✓	✓
Advertising on Rightmove, Zoopla and other portals / agent's own website	✓	✓	✓	✓
Professional photos (/ and floorplans)	(extra)	✓	✓	✓
Dealing with tenant enquiries and introductions	✓	✓	✓	✓
Viewings accompanied by agent		✓	✓	✓
Tenant referencing and credit checks	✓	✓	✓	✓
Inventory preparation		(extra)	✓	✓
EPC arranged		(extra)	✓	✓
Gas Safety Certificate (and electrical tests)		(extra)	✓	✓
Arrange utilities to be put in tenants' names			✓	✓
Supervise tenants' move-in		(extra)	✓	✓
Deposit collection and registration		(extra)	✓	✓

Prepare tenancy agreements		(extra)	✓	✓
Collect first month's rent and set up standing order		✓	✓	✓
Collect rents each month and pass on to landlords less agents' fees			✓	✓
Always be available to deal with tenants' problems				✓
Organise maintenance works as required				✓
Prepare annual rent income and expenses for accounts and tax purposes				✓
Serve notice at the end of tenancy				✓
Carry out end of tenancy property checks				✓
Release deposit appropriately after inspecting the property to decide on any deductions			✓	✓
Keep up to date with legislation and market changes	✓	✓	✓	✓

Letting Agents: The Good, The Bad and The Ugly

Every let property requires management. Some landlords, including ourselves (for the most part), choose to manage their own properties. Others may find the day-to-day management too much hassle and be too busy or remote to undertake this essential job effectively.

It's important to recognise, for each property, whether it's best to manage it yourself or get a professional agent to do so. There are many factors to be considered and several options.

I have had many encounters with letting agents over the years, some good, some bad and some indifferent. Hopefully, I've learned something in all cases, so I thought I'd share...

To give an example of an agent who impressed me: I own a property in Barnsley which is 200 miles from where I live. I am not too familiar with the area or the market. I bought the property, to put on a *rent-to-buy* scheme, below market value through a finder, and rented it to tenants who signed up to buy later.

But the tenant-buyers (a couple) split up and wanted out, so I agreed, at the agent's suggestion, to hold them to the agreement until a new buyer could be found. A price was suggested by the agent at which to market the property.

The regular updates from the agent once the property was for sale seemed to reveal scant interest. I was selling one property after another in the south, so I thought 'this is getting ridiculous', and asked him to reduce the price. But he stuck to his guns and said he thought the price was right. If I hadn't been too busy, I would probably have insisted he reduce the price, but I let it go. Every time I got an update it annoyed me! Only one person showed a keen interest but then their sale fell through. 'It's hopeless,' I thought.

I got used to ignoring the attempt to sell, since the tenants remained in situ and were paying rent. Then suddenly, out of the blue, the agent reported that the keen person who'd seen it months ago was now in a position to go ahead at the price he suggested all along.

I tell this story to illustrate the point that the agent obviously knew his area far better than I did. I'm used to the south where if a property doesn't sell quickly there's something wrong. I was prepared to reduce the price by £15,000 - £20,000 and would have done so. The moral of the story is: value your trusted agent; be prepared to respect and listen to their professional advice, knowing they do their job – in their area – all day, every day!

I have also had some bad experiences of letting agents, most notably with a small independent company where it transpired the agency owner was crooked. I had a battle to recover six properties from the agent and get my tenants' deposits handed over. It didn't help that the properties were all in Manchester, over 200 miles away. I got them back in the end and the tenants were as relieved as I was, since the agent had been most unresponsive to their requests for maintenance (and told the tenants it was the landlord's fault!).

I decided to self-manage after that and the tenants were all very understanding. Life has been much more peaceful since getting rid of the bad agent. Mind you, I have had some bad luck with maintenance costs, including a toilet fix that cost over £400 and it wasn't even replaced – Dave won't let me forget that one! I suspect if I had had a good agent, they'd have got a better price for the job, but on the whole it has worked out.

I have to say, when it comes to our local properties, the best thing for us has been self-management, especially as Dave is willing and able to devote himself to this full-time – and even manages some for a couple of my brothers. Anyone who read my first book would be aware that Dave's Diary was quite a feature – and drew many positive comments. I would have liked to include more of Dave's Diary in this book but there just wasn't enough space. Maybe one day I'll write a book devoted to Dave's Diary.

However, we do use agents for tenant-find services locally now, not least because there is more and more regulation and so much to the matter of finding good tenants, doing checks on them and producing inventories.

Choosing an Estate Agent to Sell Your Property

When choosing an agent to sell your property, there are various factors to be considered – not just price. Here are 10 tips on what to look out for:

1. **How much do they charge?** Online agents normally cost less – sometimes much less – and many charge a fixed fee, sometimes upfront. Do ask about the extent of the service, as they may require you to conduct your own viewings for example, and this is not always convenient or comfortable for many people.

2. **What professional bodies do they belong to?** Many agents belong to NAEA Propertymark and some to RICS, as well as ombudsman schemes and possibly other professional bodies.

3. **Look at their website and listings:** Some agents include floorplans while others do not; some take better photographs or have fuller details of properties. What do you think of their website and their listings?

4. **Visit the agent or have them visit you:** Are their premises, if any, attractive and well located? Does it matter to you if they are not on the high street? Do you think buyers will mind?

5. **Do you like the agent?** It is worth thinking about the saying that 'people buy people' and a likeable agent is a friend indeed.

6. **Their valuation of your property:** It is best to do your own research if you can before asking agents for their opinion, and ask a few agents so you can compare what they say. Some may try to give a flattering but unrealistically high price, while others may under-value and some will

be just right. Listen to what they say about why they are suggesting a certain price.

7. **How sensitively aware of the local market are they?** Agents who are very local and active in their remit are likely to have a more sensitive awareness of the current market conditions.

8. **Do they tend to deal in properties like yours?** Often agents are prepared to take on any property, but may have a reputation locally of being known for a particular market sector, such as the top or bottom end of the market, price-wise. It is best if your property type is well aligned with their general ethos.

9. **Do you want to instruct more than one agent?** It is possible to instruct multiple agents but many charge less for 'sole agency'. I never use more than one agent, as I feel using multiple agents can come across as desperate, which is counter-productive; but it may depend on the exact circumstances, property type and location. You decide.

10. **How proactive are they in chasing the sale along?** There can be nothing more annoying than an agent who cannot be bothered to chase all parties in order to keep the sale active. A surprisingly high percentage of property sales do fall through, often due to vendor or buyer frustration that 'nothing is happening' – don't let yours be one of them!

Selling at Auction

In certain circumstances, it can be right to sell your property at auction too. There are many physical auctions throughout the UK and investors may also buy at auction. They tend to be hunting grounds for development projects and properties in need of work; but the process can also be right when you simply need a quick and certain sale, without resorting to selling privately.

Of course, you can also buy at physical auctions too. I subscribed to the Essential Information Group www.eigpropertyauctions.co.uk for a couple of years, where you can find information about practically all UK auctions in one place, as well as further information about lots and unsold lots.

I have sold a property at auction and was quite pleased with the outcome. I also used the online auction process at www.iam-sold.co.uk to sell one of my properties in Manchester. They worked through the local estate agent branch of Your Move. I was selling through Your Move to begin with. When the property didn't sell, they suggested the online auction process which I agreed to.

Under the online auction system, the property gets marketed as 'for sale by online auction' and viewings are conducted through the local agent. Any potential buyers then submit their 'bid' (offer) knowing that other bids will be considered up to the end date of the auction (normally set to within 28 days of the start). The seller can set a reserve price for the property which is kept hidden. If at the end of the auction period there is an offer that exceeds the reserve, then the sale can go ahead. The buyer at this stage pays a reservation fee / deposit and commits to exchange contracts within 28 days and complete 28 days thereafter.

I hope that this chapter has given you some useful insights into the strategy of becoming an estate agent or letting agent, or both; and helped you to consider how it might be best for you to go about it, whether by becoming an employee at least initially, or through a franchise, or setting up your own business. We have also looked at estate agents and letting agents from the perspective of landlords and investors. If you are keen to find out more, take a look at the further resources below.

Further Reading, Resources and References

Find out more about qualifications here: www.naea.co.uk/training-qualifications/qualifications.

Also look at: www.propertymarkqualifications.co.uk/qualifications.

Find out more about joining RICS at: www.rics.org/uk.

The Property Ombudsman: www.tpos.co.uk.

See RLA (Residential Landlords Association) for their short course for letting agents: www.rla.org.uk

Glenn Ackroyd, mentioned in this chapter, is a very successful landlord with a large portfolio. He also set up EweMove Ltd, see www.EweMove.com, and was a former director of A Quick Sale Ltd. See the transcript from my interview with Glenn in Appendix III.

Book: *From Stress to Success: How to Build a Successful Business that Operates Without You*, John Paul (Nov 2017)

Author of the above-mentioned book, John Paul of Castledene at www.castledene.co.uk is a very successful letting agent.

Stuart Robinson owns and runs www.zoom995.co.uk which we've used many times and we find him most helpful as well as his staff, including Sarah Smith (in lettings), Terry Glasscoe, Jason Shackel, Kyran Fielder, Mark Luckhurst and Phil.

Estate agents' newsletter: www.estateagenttoday.co.uk.

Trade magazine for estate agents: www.thenegotiator.co.uk.

The British Franchise Association: www.thebfa.org.

Magazine about franchising: www.what-franchise.com.

International Franchise Exhibition (an annual event): www.thefranchiseshow.co.uk.

Essential Information Group for information about auctions: www.eigpropertyauctions.co.uk.

Online auctioneers: www.iam-sold.co.uk.

How does this strategy appeal to you?

Rate this strategy, on a scale from 0 - 10, for the following factors:

0 . 1 . 2 . 3 . 4 . 5 . 6 . 7 . 8 . 9 . 10 **Time**

0 . 1 . 2 . 3 . 4 . 5 . 6 . 7 . 8 . 9 . 10 **Money**

0 . 1 . 2 . 3 . 4 . 5 . 6 . 7 . 8 . 9 . 10 **Risk**

0 . 1 . 2 . 3 . 4 . 5 . 6 . 7 . 8 . 9 . 10 **Appeal**

0 . 1 . 2 . 3 . 4 . 5 . 6 . 7 . 8 . 9 . 10 **Knowledge**

0 . 1 . 2 . 3 . 4 . 5 . 6 . 7 . 8 . 9 . 10 **Aptitude**

0 . 1 . 2 . 3 . 4 . 5 . 6 . 7 . 8 . 9 . 10 **Tax**

CHAPTER 8

DEVELOPMENT

"Don't wish it was easier, wish you were better. Don't wish for less problems, wish for more skills. Don't wish for less challenges, wish for more wisdom."

Jim Rohn

Introduction

This chapter on development is not just for developers; you may be considering an investment in a project as a joint venture partner or through crowdfunding (the subject of the next chapter) or looking to become a deal sourcer. There are also many careers surrounding this subject, such as architect, builder and planner which some may be inspired to consider.

Whatever your angle of interest, there are many facets to development and many rules, regulations, restrictions and charges that might apply to any given project. It is of paramount importance that you have at least a basic grasp of what's involved before you buy a building or plot to develop, as the feasibility of the development will largely depend on the restrictions and costs.

You should also recognise the physical and practical constraints that may be present, such as access, parking, the lay of the land and what facilities and utilities are nearby to provide affordable connections. Additionally, there can be an endless stream of details that someone must make decisions on, from the foundations to the roof, from tiling to taps and every other detail too.

You will need to gather and co-ordinate your team of architects, builders and others as well as sorting finance, estimating likely timescales and having contingency funds in the event of overruns.

In this chapter, I will endeavour, within the limits of the scope of the book, to cover the basics. I will then give examples of some development projects that I have done with my brother.

But before we get started, I want to give the following wealth warning:

1. Development is an advanced strategy that often carries high levels of risk and uncertainty. It can be highly lucrative and rewarding, but with the potentially high rewards comes high risk and the potential even for bankruptcy. Never take risks you cannot afford to take.

2. Developers often use bridging finance. Be very aware of the consequences of time overruns. There can easily be delays, and you need to know how the bridging company will work with you in the event of unforeseen circumstances. Always keep financiers fully informed, or investors, if you are using crowdfunding, or joint venture partners.

3. Being an advanced strategy means that there are often many complex steps involved. You need an understanding of each step in the process to have any hope of a positive outcome.

4. I am NOT an expert. I have done a few development projects with my brother and we have used experts to support us at every step of the way – architects and other professionals.

5. Learn as much as you can and do careful due diligence on any potential site before securing it.

6. Be prepared to pay for the right experts such as architects and/or planners, builders and others to support you. Mistakes are easily made otherwise and will be expensive.

Some seem to think that development could be the logical next step for landlords who have achieved a certain level of success, as if it were like graduating in Monopoly from houses to hotels – except that in reality no such logic exists. In fact, many landlords never go on to develop property, while other people go straight into development without ever having been landlords. A small proportion, including myself and some of my successful landlord friends, have gone from landlord to developer, often doing both, but it is not inevitable.

One of the things that is appealing about development, to my mind, is that it is aligned with the political will of the country, as opposed to buy-to-let which has fallen out of favour politically, with landlords seen as hoarding properties that could have been available for first-time buyers and of pushing up prices by competing to purchase homes.

This political sea change of the past few years partly explains the popularity of development. Political favour tends to lead to better tax treatment and a more supportive regulatory environment – although I am sure many developers feel the government is not supportive enough!

Whether landlords feel unfairly treated or not, there is a housing crisis in the UK due to the simple reality of supply and demand – not enough houses are being built for the growing population. It is therefore in everyone's interests to build more houses and the government supports this point of view. Underlining this: in the November budget of 2017, the government committed to doubling the size of a key housing fund, intended to deliver infrastructure to ease the construction of new homes, to £5 billion.

What Development Encompasses

Property development includes buying land with the intention of building property either to rent or sell, or simply to gain planning permission – thereby increasing the value significantly, to sell on. Alternatively, a developer may purchase land or property once planning permission is in place, to commence work on the construction to make profits on the sale of finished units. Development encompasses a range of activities, from renovation of existing buildings to the conversion, extension or construction of buildings.

Developing property can be very creative and there are many possibilities for what you can do with either a plot of land or existing building of any type, either restoring it to its former glory or changing it. Some developers get comfortable in a certain niche, while others are more flexible in the projects they undertake, including the location.

With so many possible variations, I can only hope to list some of the most common types of projects but there is not scope to go into detail on each. I find both Your Property Network and Property Investors News magazines are very good at including articles with details of developers' projects which are always worth a look. Here is a list of some types of development project:

- Office to residential conversion (permitted development rights apply);

- Pub (and/or hotel) to mixed commercial and flats development;

- Big old building of any type (maybe working men's club) to flats;

- Barn conversions – usually to a large family home;

- Church conversions, often also to a big house;

- Shops, especially in low demand residential locations, to convert to a residential house;

- Land plots: for development of any type, within planning guidelines;

- In a crowded and expensive city such as London, developers may look at 'air rights' and seek to add storeys to buildings;

- Developers may build to rent, build to sell, build to create HMOs, or for short-term lets.

While developers organise the finance, design and building at any stage they choose to be involved in up to the point of sale, much of the work is done by professionals – architects and other experts such as surveyors and construction companies, the developer's role often being to evaluate, finance and co-ordinate the project.

There can be many stages, each carrying its own set of issues and risks. The developer must be able to adequately anticipate and carefully weigh these up, but the first thing you should appreciate is the general regulatory regime under which all development sits.

Planning Permission

Most developments can only begin once planning permission is granted (with the exception of projects that come under *permitted development rights*, as discussed below). It is worth having a basic understanding of the planning regulations and regime under which this all takes place.

National Planning Policy Framework and Local Planning Authorities

In 2012, the government brought in the National Planning Policy Framework (NPPF) which is more favourable to development than the previous set of rules. As the government's publication on this policy states:

> *The National Planning Policy Framework is a key part of the government's reforms to make the planning system less complex and more accessible. It vastly simplifies the number of policy pages about planning. The planning practice guidance to support the framework is published online and regularly updated.*

> *The framework acts as guidance for local planning authorities and decision-takers, both in drawing up plans and making decisions about planning applications.*

A Local Planning Authority (LPA) is the local authority, council or district that exercises control over planning on a local basis and it is through the LPA that planning permission must be sought. It can be a local district or borough council. The national framework as quoted above should act as guidance for local plans, but as the details of each changes relatively frequently, there can be anomalies, and local authorities can be backward in adopting national strategy. Developers with a good knowledge of the NPPF can cite their rules if a planning application is refused and goes to appeal.

It is good to know what the LPA's overall plan is for the area of your development. Every area will have a Town Plan outlining what development they may be looking to either encourage or avoid.

You can find your Local Planning Authority online and there is a wealth of information for developers at the planning portal www.planningportal.co.uk. Some LPAs have a good deal of detail about the local plans online while other sites are less informative, but you can pay them a visit in person.

Alongside the NPPF and LPA guidelines, developers should be aware of *permitted development rights*.

Permitted Development Rights

Certain types of work do not require planning permission. Your rights to carry out such works are not decided by the local authority but are derived by national statute. Bear in mind that many common projects that are permitted on houses (such as addition of a porch) will not apply to flats which will be guided by the lease; and commercial premises have other rules again.

In some areas of the country, known generally as 'designated areas', permitted development rights are more restricted. For example, if you live in:

- A Conservation Area

- A National Park

- An Area of Outstanding Natural Beauty

- A World Heritage Site or

- The Norfolk or Suffolk Broads

you will need to apply for planning permission for certain types of work which do not need an application in other areas. There are also different requirements if the property is a listed building.

Some types of development may also be given special permitted development rights from time to time, such as were recently offered for office to residential conversions.

The Town and Country Planning (General Permitted Development) (England) Order 2015

The Town and Country Planning (General Permitted Development) Order 2015 is the principal order that sets out the classes of development for which planning permission is automatically given, provided there is no restrictive condition or exemption. A reference link is given at the end of the chapter.

Article 4 Restrictions

The local planning authority may remove some permitted development rights by issuing an Article 4 direction, which means you must submit a planning application for work that normally does not need one.

Article 4 directions are made when the character of an area of acknowledged importance would be threatened. They are most common in conservation areas, but Article 4 can also be used for example to stop the creation of more HMOs in an area. You may know if your property is affected by such a direction, otherwise you can check with the local planning authority.

Green Belt

Green belt is an area around a town or city which is designated for fields and parks, and on which building is restricted. Only buildings for agricultural use or similar may be allowed but not residential or industrial buildings.

Brownfield Sites

The term brownfield site (or land) refers to derelict and under-used land. The Department for Communities and Local Government (DCLG) have created a register to provide public information about available brownfield land on a local basis. This is to speed up development of such land that could be used for new homes and to help such potential sites be easily identified. This is a new scheme. All local authorities that create a local plan should hold a register covering their region and those registers should be available soon, if not already.

Registers will include information such as:

- Site name;

- Co-ordinates of the site;

- Physical size;

- Planning status;

- Ownership;

- Housing estimate/minimum number of homes.

Contaminated Land

If you develop on contaminated land, you can claim 150% of the cost to decontaminate the land. This legislation was introduced by the Finance Act 2001 Schedule 22 to provide tax relief for contaminated land. See references section.

Planning Use Classes

Planning use classes are the legal framework which determines what any given property may be used for by its lawful occupants. In England, these are contained within the Town and Country Planning (Use Classes) Order 1987 (as amended in 2015 and 2016).

There are many different use classes each of which carries its own set of rules and regulations. You should familiarise yourself with the rules relating to the type of development you are considering. Each of the classes A to D include sub-divisions that are not listed here, but in general terms these classes include:

- Class A – shops (including some services);

- Class B – further business and industrial activities;

- Class C – hotels, hostels and dwelling houses;

- Class D – non-residential institutions;

- Sui generis: Certain uses do not fall within any use class and are considered 'sui generis'. Such uses include: theatres, larger houses in multiple occupation (more than 6 people), hostels providing no significant element of care, scrap yards, petrol filling stations and shops selling and/or displaying motor vehicles, retail warehouse clubs, nightclubs, launderettes, taxi businesses, amusement centres and casinos.

Listed Buildings

Some buildings (and other structures) are judged to be of national importance in terms of architectural or historic interest and these are included on a special register, the 'List of **Buildings** of Special Architectural or Historic Interest'. They are protected under the Planning (Listed Building and Conservation Areas) Act 1990 and there will be restrictions on works and alterations that can be carried out and on materials used.

Different classifications of listed buildings are used in different parts of the UK and the rules for works that can or cannot be done vary according to the category they are in:

- England and Wales: Grade I, Grade II* and Grade II;

- Scotland: Category A, Category B and Category C

- Northern Ireland: Grade A, Grade B+, Grade B1 and Grade B2

Whenever you are considering a building or site for purchase, it is important to find out whether it has such listed or other status that could restrict what works can be done. See references for link.

Areas of Outstanding Natural Beauty and National Parks

Another thing to be aware of when buying land or property is whether it is in an area of outstanding natural beauty (AONB). If so, the land is protected by the Countryside and Rights of Way Act 2000 (CROW Act) to conserve and enhance its natural beauty. As with listed buildings discussed above, there will be restrictions on development in such areas which are designated for conservation in recognition of their national importance.

There are also 15 national parks throughout the UK which have similar levels of protection from development, to conserve and enhance the natural and cultural heritage of the area.

Community Infrastructure Levy (CIL) and Affordable Housing Contributions

Every developer needs to be aware of and factor in the costs of the Community Infrastructure Levy, where it applies. The CIL is a charge that local authorities can set on new developments to raise funds to help with the infrastructure, facilities and services that are needed to support new homes and businesses in the area, such as schools and transport improvements. Within the national guidelines, each local authority can set out its own charges.

The charging schedule includes charges for both retail and residential uses. Your development is likely to be CIL liable if:

- The increase in floor area is 100sqm or more for retail and residential development.

- Building more than a certain minimum number of new dwellings. (Varies by LPA).

- The conversion or change of use of a building(s) is to a CIL liable development.

- The building has not been used for a continuous period of at least six months in the last three years.

The National Planning Policy Framework (NPPF) makes provision for these planning obligations, which are legally enforceable under Section 106 of the Town and Country Planning Act 1990 to mitigate the impacts of a development. Planning obligations can include:

- Requiring that the development includes some affordable housing;

- Requiring compensation (or substitute provision) for the loss of open space;

- Making a contribution to the provision of additional infrastructure to serve the development (such as a new classroom at a school) or increasing the provision of public transport.

Obligations can be direct monetary compensation, payment for other expenses or payment directly by the developer for the provision of something required by the obligation. They may also include ongoing maintenance payments.

Early discussions with the local planning authority will allow for negotiation about the imposition of planning obligations. Negotiations are usually based on viability statements and financial assessments – these documents must show that the required contribution is unaffordable and make the project financially unviable. The applicant can appeal against obligations they consider to be unreasonable.

Section 106 agreements do not generally apply to small developments of 10 homes or less, but this can vary by area and may be applied where the number of homes is as few as 5. You need to check for your area.

Sourcing and Finding Sites for Development

So far in this chapter we have looked at the rules, regulations, restrictions and levies that may apply and will have a bearing on the feasibility of a project and likelihood of getting planning permission. Now let's look at the actual process of finding and getting on with a development project.

Chapter 2 was devoted to Sourcing and there is some overlap when it comes to sourcing deals for development, but site finding – especially of raw land or derelict properties for development – is a specialist area. The key thing is to understand the potential a site may have and be able to present this well to investors who you wish to sell the deal on to.

For potential developments, three things you need to know are:

1. Price per square foot on acquisition;

2. Price per square foot on the build or refurb cost;

3. Price per square foot on the finished development: the gross development value (GDV).

The gross profit (before finance costs) can be found by subtracting points 3 – 2 – 1. You need to work backwards from (3) the estimated final value (the GDV), deducting (2) the development costs and (1) the cost of acquisition of the site, to estimate or arrive at the expected profit, to determine if the project is worthwhile.

For properties or land being considered as suitable for development or change of use, always look up the planning history on the local planning portal. If others have tried and failed to get planning permission, what makes you think that you will succeed in doing so? It can happen, but you need a clear idea of how and why that may be.

Development sites are often secured with an 'option agreement' (discussed in Chapter 2: Sourcing) while developers (or finders) often use the option period to try and get planning permission, hoping to massively uplift the value of the site. Remember that option agreements can be *assigned*, meaning you can secure the deal with an option and then sell the site on with planning permission to an investor without ever having bought it, avoiding the costs entailed in doing so.

Websites such as http://www.landinsight.io can help with site finding. Paul Higgs of Millbank Land Academy also runs courses in site finding from time to time which are highly recommended. I went along to one and found many attendees were there with a view to sourcing deals to pass on. The fees that sourcers can get were said to be around 2% of purchase price, for example:

Site Purchase Price	Fees to Finder at 2% of purchase price
£250,000	£5,000
£500,000	£10,000
£750,000	£15,000
£1,000,000	£20,000

With the potential to earn such good money as a sourcer, it makes finding a site an attractive proposition, never mind the development! This sort of fee would carry the expectation that the site was fully sourced off-market and offered exclusively; not just something that was already in the public domain for all to see.

To learn more, you might want to take a look at Millbank Academy. There are several videos featuring Paul Higgs also available on YouTube.

I also get newsletters from the Property Development Alliance chaired by Richard Little (see references).

Promap www.promap.co.uk is another useful site for developers (and land agents/finders) in assessing a site's potential. There are various types of map available, including satellite views and others.

Promap also offers links to local and planning data – you can look up if there are any previous planning permission applications (you can also do this direct at local council websites).

By getting the title for a site from Land Registry, you can look out for any covenants or restrictions that may affect the land or property.

Once you have a site or potential site to consider, what else do you need to know or do to progress your development?

Gross Development Value (GDV) and Industry Norms for Profit

When appraising the viability of a development project, developers often start with an appraisal of the Gross Development Value (GDV) which is the gross or open market value of all the properties that you are aiming to build or develop on the site. To estimate this figure, you should consider the price of comparable properties nearby and check with a professional valuer if necessary.

From this end figure, you would then work backwards to consider all the costs including CIL and affordable homes if necessary as discussed above, or particular requirements for listed buildings and such, as well as professional fees, building costs, planning fees and everything – to determine the price that should be paid for the site, to allow for sufficient profit to be made.

There is an 'industry norm' for profit on development of around 20%, to give you a benchmark.

A local estate agent may be able to help you with a rough estimate of the GDV and likely costs too, based on the 'cost per square foot' or 'square metre'. This figure may vary widely, depending on the complexity of the site, the location and other factors. Seek professional advice, for example from an architect or planning consultant (see the sections below).

You will certainly need expert help to get into the detail of costs. On projects we have done, our architect prepared a 'tender' document (an invitation for quotes) based upon a *Schedule of Rates* for each main section or location of works including electrical, plumbing, roofing, decorating, etc.

Depending on the complexity of the project, the architect may further decide to use a quantity surveyor to prepare the tender. Once the Schedule of Rates is prepared, the architect will include it in a tender document and invite either selected contractors to bid or offer it to the whole market. The architect will then go through a transparent process of evaluation and come up with a shortlist of recommendations, with comments, for the client to consider. The architect will interview the shortlist, usually 3, to clarify any points as required. You may decide to attend these meeting as we did. Then after any further clarification in writing, the architect will discuss and recommend which contractor to use and you as the client can agree or not.

When considering a site, remember to factor in the costs for demolition of derelict or unsuitable buildings, if any. You also need to account for insurance, all surveys required and other professional costs. As well as planning fees, there may be pre-application fees to pay if you wish to submit a pre-planning application (as is sometimes done, to see whether planning is likely to be forthcoming).

Finance costs if any must also be taken into account and you should always have sufficient funds for 'contingency' (an extra sum to cover the unexpected) and allow for time overruns, as things can cost more and take longer than expected!

Grants may be available in certain circumstances.

Planning Consultants, Architects and Builders

Some people appoint a planning consultant before they even buy a plot, to help determine the potential of a development. This could save you thousands of pounds by stopping you from buying a project that turns out not to be feasible. Planning consultants, as well as good architects, have full knowledge of the ever-changing planning policies that any project could be subject to.

You might alternatively speak to an architect or even a builder initially, but it's important NOT to think you can do everything by yourself if you are inexperienced and unqualified. If there's one thing I want to get across in this chapter, it is this!

I learned from my brother, Antony, who has been most instrumental in bringing about our successful developments, that it is so important to employ experts and to recognise your own limitations. There are so many experts you can call upon depending on the project, each invaluable if chosen well.

Do not underestimate the complexities of construction either and use a good construction firm; there is a whole language around building, first fix, second fix... I'm not even going to go there!

Start by using a good architect or planning consultant to help submit your planning application and you will have a much higher chance of success than if you try to do it yourself or skimp on this cost. We used a good local architect for all our developments.

Local authorities work to guidelines for how long it takes to determine planning applications, and this should normally be 10-12 weeks for more straightforward plans. There can be some to-ing and fro-ing as the council advise of amendments they require to the plans.

Every case is different, and you should expect the whole process to take potentially much longer from when you first instruct an architect to when hopefully you get your planning permission.

Funding for Development Deals

Development projects are often undertaken with the help of borrowed money. Given the potential for high returns, this leverage can escalate your wealth rapidly but there are risks in borrowing, particularly for development, and the cost of borrowing will reflect the level of risk involved.

The type of finance should suit the situation and can include bridging finance and bank finance, or alternatively crowdfunding, as will be discussed in more detail in the next chapter.

See an independent financial advisor about your finance needs, or look into crowdfunding as an alternative, according to the situation. See also the Finance chapter for more information.

A key point I would like to make is that you should always have a contingency fund (extra money set aside) in case costs end up being more than expected as can easily happen due to unforeseen complications. Also think of contingency in terms of time. The projects that my brother and I have done all took far longer than anticipated. We did not borrow money, but it could get expensive or lead to difficulties if you are on expensive bridging not intended for such long-term use.

Our Projects

My brother Antony and I have done several development projects jointly over the past few years. Here is a brief look at three of our biggest projects to date, the latest of which is ongoing.

Victoria House in Shropshire

Front View of Victoria House:

Victoria House was a derelict pub with planning permission for 6 flats and 2 commercial units, from a developer who planned to start the project but never had the resources or capability.

We had heard that there might be grants available and after consulting the best local architect, found that it was possible to create several more flats than the original developer had planned, plus one more commercial unit.

One of the complications with this property is that it is grade II listed, which we knew would present challenges regarding certain aspects of the work, but with the guidance from our architect, we were confident that these issues could be overcome.

Our architect drew up plans for 11 flats with 3 commercial units on the ground floor (which could be re-configured to create one large unit if required). The property is very deep, with one of the commercial units and access to all the residential flats being in the walkway to the left-hand side of the frontage.

We went ahead and purchased the property in May 2014 and eventually got the planning permission to go ahead with the project.

One of the challenges of the grade II listed status was that the council were reluctant to grant permission for the original pub windows to be changed, but with strong support from the local Chamber of Commerce, we managed to get this restriction lifted in favour of the normal shop front windows which are much better for most businesses.

Key to the success of this project was that we managed to get two grants.

The first grant was for the commercial units, on provision that it would help in the regeneration of the High Street and would create jobs for local people.

The second grant was given on condition that we make the flats available as affordable rented units. To meet with this condition, we then leased all the residential flats to a housing association.

We were exempt from the Community Infrastructure Levy (CIL) and the Affordable Homes charges that would have been due at a cost of £38,000 for the former and £20,000 for the latter because we signed up under the grant conditions to lease the residential flats as affordable housing units.

The property comes with a decent-sized car park which we also developed, and it now produces an additional income.

The figures for Victoria House are:

Purchase Price:	£125,000
Net Refurbishment Costs after Grants	£557,000
Total Costs:	£682,000
Estimated GDV:	£830,000
Estimated Capital Gain	21.70%
Gross Yield	10.77%

Southlawns in Rhyl

Antony and I acquired the property in Rhyl in June 2012. It also dates back to Victorian times, when it was originally a small private school. When we acquired the property, the works were part done, to a reasonable standard. There was still some work required to 2 of the flats, plus external work including a collapsed drain and failing external metal fire staircase.

The final development consisted of 7 self-contained flats with their own utilities, meaning no disputes about who is using too much electricity or water.

Southlawns, Rhyl: front and side views

We employ a small local letting agent to manage the rentals and have always managed to attract a high quality of tenants as we keep the maintenance of the building to the highest of standards. This is also a grade II listed building with some delightful period features including a very ornate banister.

Despite being configured as seven self-contained flats, the properties remain on the one title, so it is treated as a licensable HMO by the local council of Rhyl, in Wales. We chose not to split the title as we wanted to keep the whole property and did not want to end up with potential problems that might arise if there were several piecemeal owners.

The property, as you can see from the photographs, has been substantially extended over the years, with several extensions being added. While the main front portion of the building was relatively straightforward to configure into flats, the later extended areas to the back presented rather more challenges both in terms of the layout and some of the build quality of the extensions.

We bought the place for cash and had the cash to complete the remaining works too, so we had no finance costs to worry about.

The figures for Southlawns, Rhyl are:

Purchase Price:	£250,000
Refurbishment Costs	£80,000
Total Costs:	£330,000
Estimated GDV:	£465,000
Estimated Capital Gain	40.90%
Gross Yield	10.77%

Forewood Wells, Kent (AONB)

Photo of The Reservoir Before:

Photo of the Reservoir After (Design of what it will look like when built):

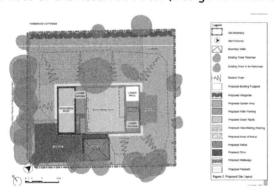

This project which we bought in January 2011 consists of a 32-acre site in rural Kent, in an Area of Outstanding Natural Beauty (the AOBN being High Weald). Antony and I have joint ventured on this one with the builder-developer who originally found the site and saw its potential. We put up the money.

The site consists of three main parts: there is a Pump House which was derelict and for which we got planning permission for a holiday home only: this has been done, and the deal was that this part of the project was parcelled off to and sold to our JV partner Keith for 2/3rd of the value. We have therefore made a 100% return on our original investment.

The figures for the Pump House are:

Purchase Price of Whole Site	£125,000
Cost to get Planning Permission for Pump House	£50,000
Total Costs:	£175,000
Sale of Pump House to JV Partner	£250,000
Capital Gain	60.00%

The photos above are of the most exciting part of the site: a very old, disused, Victorian reservoir which dates from March 1853, with its capacity expanded in 1924. A big hole in the ground with potential! This reservoir is of historical and local architectural interest but is a non-designated heritage structure.

It helped having no finance costs to worry about, as the many stages, issues, surveys, site clearance and all sorts of delays meant that it took years to finally, in 2017, get planning permission for a very large house.

With it being an AONB, the house has to be upside down and largely below ground level, to minimise the visual impact on the surrounding countryside and the few neighbours in houses nearby. The design is very complex because of this, and we believe there is a chance that *Grand Designs* could be interested in following this development!

We are at this point in time weighing up whether to go ahead with the actual building of the development, or to sell it on with the planning permission as it is. There are still some matters to be ironed out regarding the access.

If we sell with just planning permission, this money will be pure profit. If we decide to develop, we will have to weigh up the potential costs v value. Then there is the final 24 acres of land that we can sell. Watch this space.

The figures for the Reservoir are:

Cost to obtain Planning Permission:	£28,000
Estimated sale price of Plot with PP	£300,000
Estimated Capital Gain	971.70%

The remaining 24 acres of Land are conservatively valued at around £24,000.

Further Reading, Resources and References

The Government's National Planning Policy Framework: https://www.gov.uk/government/publications/national-planning-policy-framework--2

Planning Portal has a wealth of information for developers, including this article about brownfield sites: https://www.planningportal.co.uk/info/200130/common_projects/49/self-build_homes/4

Planning guidance: https://www.gov.uk/government/collections/planning-practice-guidance.

The Town and Country Planning Order 2015: http://www.legislation.gov.uk/uksi/2015/596/contents/made.

Article about tax relief compensation for decontaminating land for development: http://www.capitalallowancesdirect.com/contaminated-land.

Planning use classes: http://www.legislation.gov.uk/uksi/1987/764/contents/made.

Further information about listed buildings: https://ecab.planningportal.co.uk/uploads/1app/guidance/guidance_note-listed_building_consent.pdf

Websites such as http://www.landinsight.io can help with site finding.

Paul Higgs of Millbank Land Academy runs courses in development site finding: www.millbanklandacademy.co.uk.

Promap also helps with assessing land and development sites: www.promap.co.uk.

Property Development Alliance, Richard Little:
www.propertydevelopmentalliance.com.

Homebuilding and Renovating magazine is available in newsagents, also online at https://www.homebuilding.co.uk. Mainly geared towards people who are looking to self-build or do big extensions and renovations. Has many 'user-friendly' articles for inexperienced developers.

Property magazines that regularly have articles detailing specific development projects, alongside a range of quality articles on all things property:

Your Property Network: www.yourpropertynetwork.co.uk.

Property Investor News: www.property-investor-news.com.

How does this strategy appeal to you?

Rate this strategy, on a scale from 0 - 10, for the following factors:

0 . 1 . 2 . 3 . 4 . 5 . 6 . 7 . 8 . 9 . 10   **Time**

0 . 1 . 2 . 3 . 4 . 5 . 6 . 7 . 8 . 9 . 10   **Money**

0 . 1 . 2 . 3 . 4 . 5 . 6 . 7 . 8 . 9 . 10   **Risk**

0 . 1 . 2 . 3 . 4 . 5 . 6 . 7 . 8 . 9 . 10   **Appeal**

0 . 1 . 2 . 3 . 4 . 5 . 6 . 7 . 8 . 9 . 10   **Knowledge**

0 . 1 . 2 . 3 . 4 . 5 . 6 . 7 . 8 . 9 . 10   **Aptitude**

0 . 1 . 2 . 3 . 4 . 5 . 6 . 7 . 8 . 9 . 10   **Tax**

CHAPTER 9

CROWDFUNDING

"As an investor you have the opportunity to pick and choose projects that most resonate with you and deliver the best returns or rewards. As a borrower, you now have access to potentially millions of investors. On both sides, the opportunity is immense. Embrace it!"

Davin Poonwassie

Introduction

Crowdfunding forms part of *the alternative finance market*. It provides a way for people, organisations and businesses, including business startups, to raise money through online portals called crowdfunding platforms, to finance or refinance their activities, and for investors to provide that money. The business or individual seeking finance present their project via the platform to attract loans or investment from the crowd.

Whilst the sector has seen explosive growth in recent years, and even been referred to as "a movement", peer-to-peer lending began in 2005 with Zopa, who focussed on individual consumer lending. The market has since mushroomed to include a range of platforms offering not just consumer loans but also property lending and a range of small to medium (SME) business financing options.

The potential rates of return, while carrying risk, have a fairly obvious appeal to investors given the low interest rates available to savers. The tightening up of bank lending in recent years has also made crowdfunding extra attractive for those seeking funds for their projects too.

In December 2017, the 4th UK Alternative Finance Industry Report was published, the study being undertaken jointly by the University of Cambridge Centre for Alternative Finance and the CME Group Foundation. (See reference section for link to the report.) It was reported that the UK alternative finance industry grew to £3.3 billion. This was a £1.1 billion (50%) increase on the £2.2 billion raised in 2015.

The Peer-to-Peer Property Lending model was only categorised as an independent model from 2015 onward and has proven to be one of the largest drivers of the UK's alternative finance industry. It is the third largest model by volume, generating £1.147 billion in 2016, which represents an 88% annual increase.

Crowdfunding should be looked at in conjunction with other more traditional forms of finance (as considered in the earlier chapter on finance) to weigh up the costs and benefits.

Many property deals offered for crowdfunding have a focus on development or refurbishment and/or planning gain, although some may be medium term and include a period of renting out the property to benefit from expected capital appreciation over time.

Financial Conduct Authority (FCA)

The FCA is responsible for regulating loan-based and equity-based forms of crowdfunding in the UK. These are the two forms of crowdfunding that are relevant to property and which will be further discussed in this chapter. They publish reports and give their views here: https://www.fca.org.uk/consumers/crowdfunding.

Other types of crowdfunding, which the FCA don't regulate, include donation-based crowdfunding whereby people give money to enterprises or organisations they want to support; and pre-payment or rewards-based crowdfunding, where people give money in return for a reward, service or product such as concert tickets, an innovative product, or a computer game for example.

We will examine the potential of property-related alternative finance for both borrowers (or fundraisers) and investors (or funders), as well as the platforms themselves, asking what it takes to get registered with the FCA as a platform provider.

There are in total around 98 registered crowdfunding platforms in the UK, according to published research by the FCA. Property is just one sector among them. I provide a list of property-related platforms of which I am aware, later in the chapter.

Most property crowdfunding platforms charge fees of between 3%-5% to borrowers who are raising the funds but do not charge fees to investors, although you should check.

We will now look at some of the property crowdfunding platforms that I have personally encountered and invested through:

Simple Crowdfunding

I have invested in several projects with Simple Crowdfunding www.simplecrowdfunding.co.uk and have personally met the founders, Davin and Atuksha Poonwassie, who are most helpful and have written a book, *Simple Crowdfunding*, as listed in the Resources section.

Davin completed a questionnaire about himself as part of my research for this strategy, and I include a copy of at www.propertyinvestingstrategies.co.uk. Davin describes himself as **"a property and fintech entrepreneur"**. I found this definition of the term fintech on Wikipedia:

> *"The most comprehensive scientific study on the definition of fintech concludes that 'fintech is a new financial industry that applies technology to improve financial activities.' FinTech is the new applications, processes, products, or business models in the financial services industry, composed of one or more complementary financial services and provided as an end-to-end process via the internet."*

Simple Crowdfunding has peer-to-peer lending and equity projects sitting side by side on the platform. They allow investing using the Innovative Finance ISA (IFISA) wrapper for eligible projects, allowing for tax-free property investing.

Some projects offer a "learn whilst investing" element whereby investors can learn from fundraisers throughout the lifetime of the project. The platform also allows and helps fundraisers to build their brand online.

John Corey

John Corey of https://www.propertyfortress.com has also helped me to learn more about property crowdfunding. John set up a crowdfunding mastermind programme which I joined for a time. It is mainly geared towards people who are considering bringing deals to the crowd and who would like support.

John coined the phrase **"invest to learn"**. As John says, you could easily pay £100-£500 for a one-day property educational event, yet joining a crowdfunding deal effectively gives you access to learn about development and all the available documentation. Some crowdfunded deals also offer webinars at key stages, giving investors further opportunities to learn. John acts as a lead investor when invited by fundraisers, to help deliver this educational element to investors.

Crowd With Us

I have also met some of the team behind Crowd With Us https://www. crowdwithus.london, including Thor Portess and Paul Higgs (whose land sourcing event I attended, as mentioned in Chapter 8 on Development).

The platform offers deals that are brought to the crowd by the Crowd With Us (CWU) team – hence the name. The deals are presented using one of two simple models that they offer:

Model 1: Buy-to-let:

"We find a suitable property and split the buying costs into shares. CWU receives 50% of the shares, in exchange for the directors personally guaranteeing mortgage finance. The remaining shares are offered to the crowd.

The property will be sold in 5 years providing it has gone up by at least 50% in value in relation to the total costs of acquiring the property. If the property has increased by 50% in value at any point with respect to the total acquisition costs in less than 5 years, it will be sold at that point."

Model 2: Loan notes:

"The loan funds are invested into a specific property project such as property development where the property is going to be either: (1) Sold; or (2) Rented and then sold.

This model generally applies to more short-term projects which may carry higher risk than a straightforward buy-to-let rental investment depending on the scenario. Of course, these risks are managed, and details can be found in the Term Sheet for the specific project."

Interesting that CWU describe their loan-based deals as riskier than the equity-based deals, as the latter have an element of buy-to-let which gives them added safety arguably compared to some other equity-based models.

Crowd Property

The Crowd Property platform at https://www.crowdproperty.com was set up by Simon Zutshi, a well-known property educator and author, who also runs the Property Investors Network. Deals are offered on a loan basis, usually at this time (from a look at the site) offering around 8% per annum returns to investors. Crowd Property has this to say about the deals on its site:

> "We do everything we possibly can to make sure every project on CrowdProperty is a reliable opportunity for our lenders. As well as completing extensive due diligence before approving a project, we

also make sure we have the first legal charge over a property just in case anything doesn't go to plan. Our primary concern is making sure that our lenders' loans are secure, but as with all loans for property our expertise does not absolve the lender from risk. We actively encourage all of our lenders to complete their own research or seek advice from an Independent Financial Adviser if they are ever unsure about funding a project."

Crowd Property itself recently raised funds to help grow their business, which is rather fitting! I learned of the raise via Simon's mailing list and decided to invest. The equity-based funds were raised through Seedrs, one of the biggest and best-known general crowdfunding platforms.

Loan-Based Crowdfunding (P2P)

Also known as 'peer-to-peer lending' (P2P), loan-based crowdfunding allows consumers to lend money in return for interest payments and a repayment of capital at the end of the investment period, normally a fixed term. Some of the most well-established peer-to-peer lending platforms, such as Zopa or Seedrs, give ratings to borrowers often in accordance with their credit rating profile, with varying rates of return to match these being offered to lenders. When I looked at Zopa while writing this chapter, I found there is a waiting list to be an investor!

The rate of return on offer is normally higher than investors could find with traditional savings such as banks and bonds, but it should be remembered that there is risk involved and capital is not protected in the same way (see FCA section below). In property, crowdfunded loans may be secured by a charge against the property.

According to Nesta, 44% of UK retail investors would like to increase their exposure to the property market, not only through their home, but also in other ways such as investing through peer-to-peer lenders.

Nesta reported in 2015 that peer-to-peer lending for property grew to £609 million, amounting to 41% of the total volume of P2P loans. Overall, P2P real estate lending financed over 600 commercial and residential developments in the UK in 2015, mostly by small to medium-sized property developers. A variety of models and products are offered, with the length of investment varying from short-term (12 - 18 months) to longer term (3 - 5 years) and the purpose of loans varying too, as well as expected exits.

In their 2015 survey, Nesta found that the average acceptance rate for P2P property loan applications was 27.5%. The average size of loans was £522,333 with an average of 490 lenders.

It is expected that with the introduction of the IFISA (see below) the numbers investing will substantially increase.

IFISA

Within loan-based crowdfunding, the **Innovative Finance ISA** (IFISA) was introduced on 6th April 2016 to allow individuals to earn tax-free interest on peer-to-peer (P2P) lending activities.

An ISA is a savings and investment account that you never pay tax on, making it attractive to many. You can save up to a maximum of £20,000 in 2017/18 (the Junior ISA allowance for investing for children is £4,128). This can be in a cash ISA, a stocks & shares ISA, an innovative finance ISA, a Help to Buy ISA, a Lifetime ISA or a mixture of all of them.

While you can invest in multiple P2P deals, you can only open an IFISA with one platform in a given tax year.

Equity-Based Crowdfunding

Consumers invest directly or indirectly in new or established businesses by buying investments such as shares or debentures.

Nesta report that in 2015, equity-based crowdfunding for property raised £87 million in total for 174 fundraisers' development projects. Growth rates increased rapidly over the year, indicating that equity-based crowdfunding for property has the potential to become a substantial segment within the UK alternative finance industry, as it has in other markets such as the United States.

Though growth rates increased, only 2.9% of deals that applied were accepted onto platforms, although the success rate for funding was 87% for those that made it onto a platform; the average deal size was £820,042, with an average of 150 investors participating per deal.

Becoming a Crowdfunding Investor

The first thing you need to do is register with a platform before you can see any details beyond a brief outline of deals available, or indeed invest. I found registering a fairly simple process but it's worth further discussion before we move on, about why it is necessary and what's required.

Registering as an Investor

When you look at crowdfunding platforms, you will be able to see a summary of deals available to invest in and some that have already been funded. However, you will not have access to further details and documents, or be able to invest, unless you register with the site first.

Most sites will ask you to declare your financial status, in keeping with FCA rules which include marketing restrictions. Firms can only make direct offer promotions to retail customers who meet certain criteria, so you will be asked to verify if you fit into one of the required categories:

- Those who qualify as high net worth or sophisticated investors;

- Those who confirm they will invest less than 10% of their net assets in this type of security;

- Those who take independent regulated advice.

In addition, you will have to acknowledge an understanding of the implications of being treated as a High Net Worth Individual or Sophisticated Investor, including:

- The ability to receive financial promotions that may not have been approved by a firm regulated by the Financial Conduct Authority (FCA) and whose content may not conform to FCA rules.

- The loss of the right to complain to the Financial Conduct Authority or the Financial Ombudsman Scheme.

- The loss of the right to seek compensation from the Financial Services Compensation Scheme.

All this may be seem daunting, but it is intended to help protect consumers from taking part in risky investments that they may not fully understand. Inversely, if you do register as an investor on a crowdfunding platform, it is assumed that you do understand the risks and can afford to take them.

Self-Certified Sophisticated Investor Requirements

To qualify as a self-certified sophisticated investor, you should be able to meet one of these criteria:

- You have been a member of a network or syndicate of business angels for at least six months before the date of self-certification; or

- Have made more than one investment in an unlisted company in the two years before the date of self-certification; or

- Work in a professional capacity in the private equity sector for financing small and medium enterprises (SMEs) in the two years before the date of self-certification; or

- Been a director in the two years prior to self-certification of a company with annual turnover of £1 million or more.

Certified High Net Worth Individual Requirements

To certify that you are a high net worth individual, you should be able to meet one of these criteria:

- Having an annual income of £100,000 or more during the year immediately preceding the date of self-certification; or

- Having net assets of £250,000 or more – not including a primary residence, rights under an insurance contract or pension or termination benefits.

According to a report commission by Knight Frank, London is the city with the highest number of HNWIs as of December 2016, with New York in second place. (In the US, a high net worth individual is defined as someone with a net worth over $1 million US dollars.)

So Now You Can Invest

Once registered, you will be able to see all the available documents and details for each of the deals, to help you make an informed choice about what to invest in.

I have found that the amount of detail on offer varies as does the presentation, some being clearer than others. Some presentations are too sparse, or at the other extreme go into detail that only an accountant would enjoy reading. Generally, there should be a business plan which is clear and well-presented but palatable.

Of course, the main thing that investors want to know is: what are the expected returns, the timeframe of the investment, as well as what security is on offer.

Loan-based investments may offer a first charge on the property, while equity-based investments offer shares in the company or SPV (special purpose vehicle – a company set up just for the investment in question). The returns on loan-based investments tend to be much lower, reflecting the lower risk and may be a fixed rate of interest (but note your capital is still at risk).

The returns on equity-based investments may appear a lot more, but remember this reflects the greater risk.

The highest risk investments seem to be "planning gain" type deals, which depend on planning gain for the plot to have any uplift in value and investors can lose everything if the planning application fails. Having said that, I took part in a planning gain deal where the fundraiser managed to sell on the plot at auction despite no planning having been gained and investors did get their money back with a 10% uplift.

Which brings me to the next point: a key factor when considering investments is the expected exit for investors and whether the developer has a 'Plan B' should the preferred exit not be achieved.

You should also look at the developer or fundraiser:

- How experienced is the developer?

- Do they seem capable of dealing with the unexpected?

- Do some due diligence by googling their name.

- Try looking them up at Companies House to see what track record they have of running companies. www.companieshouse.gov.uk.

- Or look them up via www.duedil.com.

As mentioned earlier, some investments may come with the opportunity to find out more through webinars and sometimes even site visits which can be fun, but do not be unduly swayed by the personalities involved; use such events to your advantage, not to be taken in.

When you find an investment that you are fully satisfied you wish to invest in, you can then offer through the site how much you want to invest and will be called on to submit this sum to the platform. The platform should have a separate client or escrow account for investors' funds. Assuming the deal attracts sufficient total funds in time for the raise, it will then be able to go ahead. At that stage you will be asked to confirm that you are happy to go ahead and to sign the appropriate agreement. You are now a crowdfunding investor!

Raising Money for Your Project From the Crowd

If you wish to borrow from the crowd, you need to be aware of the process and what will be required. You should also consider whether the type of deal and the returns you are prepared to offer match the expectations of investors and whether you have the right sort of credibility to attract investors. You should also take steps if possible to attract at least some investment from your own crowd, but remember, primarily the deal needs to stack well for investors. While you need to be seen as capable and trustworthy, it's not all about you. You also need to be careful and take advice from the platform about what you can or can't do with regards to promotion of your deal as this is a highly regulated activity and you are not allowed to advertise or promote the details of the deal.

A very good place to start is to look at the platforms that appeal to you and see what other deals are being offered. Of course, you first need to ascertain whether the platform allows for loan-based, equity-based or IFISA deals, whichever you plan to offer. Get a feel for the terms and the returns that other borrowers are offering, and see what the uptake is.

Platforms vary on the exact documentation that they will require of you, both in terms of the type and degree of detail. You should welcome a fair level of scrutiny in this respect as it shows integrity of the site and could help you to submit a better offering. The most common documentation that investors will want to see includes:

- A business plan for the deal;

- Financial statements;

- Tax returns;

- Legal documents;

- Loan repayment plan;

- Security;

- Other documents which may include for example your credit report.

The Business Plan

The main document that you must submit and which investors will want to read is the business plan. This should include details of the opportunity, giving the reasons for the raise, details of the project with photographs, floor plans and a map, your team's background and experience, the history of the company or SPV (*special purpose vehicle*, meaning a company formed just for the one project), what security is offered and so on.

Normally loan-based deals offer investors a first charge on the property and fixed rate of return, which may be paid either regularly or rolled up until the end of the investment. Equity-based deals offer shares in the company, and the details of this should be outlined together with what percentage of profits will be shared with investors.

The platform hosts will discuss with you what you are allowed or not allowed to do or say in your promotion, either on the site or elsewhere (such as on social media). Hint: you are not allowed to promote details on social media or do anything that could be construed as trying to entice consumers to invest.

Once you have got all your documents uploaded to the platform, the hosts will check them with you prior to approval. When ready, your deal can go live, investors will be able to invest, and assuming the deal raises sufficient funds, then the deal can go ahead: Congratulations, you are a crowdfunder!

Crowdfunding for Platform Hosts

You might be interested in asking what it takes to get registered as a platform provider. According to the authorising body, the FCA, they require applicants to take the following steps:

- Submit a suitable and detailed regulatory business plan setting out the planned activities (and related risks), budget and resources (human, systems and capital).

- Have adequate non-financial resources (ie the management board has adequate knowledge and experience of financial regulation).

- Have adequate financial resources when submitting the application (ie not looking at future fundraising to reach the requirement).

- Have a website that is either up-and-running or at a suitably advanced stage to demonstrate how it will operate should the firm be authorised.

- Understand the requirement for FCA authorisation and the permission profile for which they wish to apply.

The FCA has set up a support hub for businesses that are looking to introduce such financial services to the market, including when they need assistance with an application for authorisation or variation of permission.

Examples of Crowdfunding Deals

Here are some examples of *previous* (ie no longer available) crowdfunding deals of various deal structures, for illustrative purposes only, of the sorts of structure, timescales and returns that you might expect to typically find – although each deal varies and sites may offer a variety or favour specific models:

Example 1: A Planning Gain Deal

This was an actual deal that I have recently invested in through Simple Crowdfunding. I have met the people behind the deal, so that helped me to have the confidence to invest.

THE OPPORTUNITY

Project Summary – Planning gain
Share Price – £100
Raise Amount – £10,000 to £35,000
Number of Shares Issued – 100 to 350
Projected Return on Investment – 50%*
Expected Completion Timescale – 6 to 8 months

*This is a high-risk, potentially high-return project. If initial planning is not obtained, we will return to the Local Planning Authority considering their reasons for refusal. We shall also look to appeal the decision should we believe it prudent to do so, at no cost to investors. If overall planning is not granted after appeal, the option on the site will not be exercised and investors will lose their whole investment.

THE PROJECT

This project involves acquiring a plot of land on a single freehold basis, with the aim of achieving planning for a mixed use of 9 commercial units and 24 residential flats. The site is legally secured with an option agreement and initial discussions with the planning department have been met with positive feedback.

We have a network of agents who will be working on agreement to lease on the commercial units before we build the building out.

By obtaining this planning we shall be increasing the land value of the site considerably, and we will intend to build the site out after this initial planning gain. We might look to have another raise for the next stage of development.

The exit for investors will be development finance for the build phase. Funds raised will pay for the planning application and the raise is underwritten by the company. The minimum raise is £10,000. The fundraisers will fund any remaining funds.

All figures have been prepared by the developers on the basis of information available to them and their past experience of similar projects. As with all investments, returns are not guaranteed.

Example 2: An IFISA Refurbishment Deal

This is another deal I have invested in through Simple Crowdfunding. This one is presented on a loan basis and offered as an IFISA (described in an earlier section). I also met the person behind the deal, who was a member of the same mastermind group, prior to bringing this deal to market.

LOAN TERMS

Summary: A dated 3-bed terraced house (via auction) in need of refurbishment purchased for £39,999. The loan is for 75% of the purchase price. There are no structural works, development or planning issues. It is a standard refurbishment and modernisation.

Investment type: Loan (IF ISA applicable)

Raise amount: £25,000 (min) to £30,000 (max)

Interest payment: 0.5% per month.

Interest payment terms: Paid monthly in arrears for the calendar month on the 10th day of the following month

Projected loan start date: 12th November 2017

Loan term: For up to 15 months repayable on refinance but subject to a minimum of 12 months interest payments even if paid back early

Minimum investment: £500

Security: First charge over the property will be taken on behalf of the lenders

Interest apportionment: Where funds are received from the 1st to the 15th of the month, pro-rata payment 10 days after month end. Where funds are received from the 16th to month end, the pro-rata amount is added to the following month's payment.

Note: As the project progresses there may be another raise on this deal to fund some of the refurbishment works. If this occurs, a second charge will be offered that will sit behind the first charge offered here.

THE PROJECT

This is an opportunity to invest in a refurbishment project in Northumberland. The developer has purchased a large 3-bedroom, mid-terraced house of standard construction in an area of good rental demand by LHA tenants. It is cosmetically dated but otherwise structurally sound.

Due to the purchase price and condition it is currently unmortgageable, which is why the developer has turned to peer-to-peer lending. The funds will be used for the (partial) acquisition cost of this property. The plan is to add value through a full refurbishment and modernisation before tenanting and refinancing it for a long-term hold.

There is no structural work, alterations or additions, permitted development or planning gains related to this project. This is a standard refurbishment project and is typical of the types of projects managed by this developer previously.

Example 3: An Equity-Based Deal

Remember, this is a past deal, no longer available for investment. I did not invest in this deal, as it was offered before I started looking, but I give it here as an example of an equity deal structure. Again, this one was offered on the Simple Crowdfunding platform.

THE OPPORTUNITY

Project Summary – Development comprising four luxury townhouses in London
Share Price – £2,000
Raise Amount – £1 Million - £2 Million
Number of Shares Issued – 500 - 1,000
Projected Return on Investment – 50%
Expected Completion Date – October 2018

THE PROJECT

This is a development comprising four luxury townhouses in London. The developers have a contract to develop the freehold site, which is owned by a charity. They will fund the development of the four residential units and in return have a contract for sale of two units (total approximately 6000 sq ft net internal area). Planning permission has been granted by the local council to demolish the existing buildings and construct 4 x 4-bedroom 3-storey new homes each with basement rooms, roof terraces at the rear and two parking spaces.

The site consists of a main two-storey building with a small basement, and single-storey outbuildings along its boundary with the rear gardens of houses. The buildings are in a poor state of disrepair and have been vacant for a number of years. The last lawful use of the site was for the purposes of a school. The surrounding area is entirely residential in character.

Example 4: Equity-Based Medium Term Buy-to-Let

This example is from the CrowdWithUs platform mentioned earlier in this chapter. This was a buy-to-let equity style investment as described earlier:

Enfield, 4-bed house

Bought Sept 2013

Price: £294,000

Refurbishment & Costs: £37,000

Estimated value 2017: £530,000

Growth: £199,000 in 3.42 years

Percentage gain 68% in 3.42 years

All the examples above gave further details, but I've given summaries for illustrative purposes only. None of the deals shown are available; they were all fully funded within the time limits set for the raise.

There follows a list of all the property-focused crowdfunding platforms of which I am aware at this time:

List of Property-Related Crowdfunding Platforms

Here is an alphabetical list of UK-based **property-related** crowdfunding websites of which I am aware (some are hybrids, offering other types of investment alongside property). The list is not necessarily complete or accurate. Note that there are many other crowdfunding sites in addition to this which are not property related. The Nesta report (see Resources) includes a list of many more varied sites.

- AssetzCapital: https://www.assetzcapital.co.uk

- BridgeCrowd: https://www.thebridgecrowd.com

- CrowdLords: https://www.crowdlords.com

- CrowdProperty: https://www.crowdproperty.com

- CrowdWithUs: https://www.crowdwithus.london

- LandBay: https://landbay.co.uk

- LandlordInvest: https://landlordinvest.com

- Propnology: https://www.propnology.co.uk

- SimpleCrowdfunding: www.simplecrowdfunding.co.uk

- The House Crowd: https://www.thehousecrowd.com

- U-Own: https://www.uown.co

Further Reading, Resources and References

The crowdfunding platforms further discussed in this chapter:

- **SimpleCrowdfunding:** www.simplecrowdfunding.co.uk

- **CrowdWithUs**: https://www.crowdwithus.london

- **CrowdProperty**: https://www.crowdproperty.com

Book: *Simple Crowdfunding*, Davin and Atuksha Poonwassie, 2015

UK Alternative Finance Industry Report was published, the study being undertaken jointly by the University of Cambridge Centre for Alternative Finance and the CME Group Foundation: https://www.jbs.cam.ac.uk/faculty-research/centres/alternative-finance/publications/entrenching-innovation/#.Wlys1E1LFMu

FCA report: https://www.fca.org.uk/consumers/crowdfunding

Knight Frank Wealth Report: http://www.knightfrank.com/wealthreport/2017/download.aspx

How does this strategy appeal to you?

Rate this strategy, on a scale from 0 - 10, for the following factors:

0 . 1 . 2 . 3 . 4 . 5 . 6 . 7 . 8 . 9 . 10   **Time**

0 . 1 . 2 . 3 . 4 . 5 . 6 . 7 . 8 . 9 . 10   **Money**

0 . 1 . 2 . 3 . 4 . 5 . 6 . 7 . 8 . 9 . 10   **Risk**

0 . 1 . 2 . 3 . 4 . 5 . 6 . 7 . 8 . 9 . 10   **Appeal**

0 . 1 . 2 . 3 . 4 . 5 . 6 . 7 . 8 . 9 . 10   **Knowledge**

0 . 1 . 2 . 3 . 4 . 5 . 6 . 7 . 8 . 9 . 10   **Aptitude**

0 . 1 . 2 . 3 . 4 . 5 . 6 . 7 . 8 . 9 . 10   **Tax**

CHAPTER 10

FINANCE

"Whether you think you can or you think you can't, you're probably right."

Henry Ford

Introduction

Finance is like a thread that runs through everything in property, along with tax.

You should always consider finance in the light of tax, and vice versa, particularly since the introduction of tax measures to limit mortgage interest to a tax credit of 20%, as discussed in the chapter on tax and elsewhere. In general terms, this makes it unfavourable from a tax point of view to have high leverage for higher rate taxpayers buying in individual names. Circumstances differ, and you should always seek personal tax and mortgage advice. I am not a tax or financial advisor, so to give a disclaimer – anything I say should not be relied upon nor construed as financial advice.

In this chapter I introduce the types of finance available for various property projects, from buy-to-let to development and everything in between. All successful property investors and developers are good planners, and getting the right finance in place is a crucial ingredient in property success, whether you're buying to develop, or growing your rental portfolio.

The table below gives a broad look at the most common types of finance available and the projects they are most suited to. While there are many variations, most finance is either broadly buy-to-let (shown in green in the table) or of a development nature (shown in blue), or for commercial property (grey) There are many variants. You may also joint venture or use crowdfunding.

This chapter will look at each of the main types of finance, as well as considering lender and regulatory requirements, mortgage advisors and your credit rating.

Table of Finance for Various Types of Property Project:

Project Type:	BTL habitable	Refurb to Let (to make habitable)	Refurb to sell	Heavy Refurb	Build from Ground	Conversion / Commercial / Resi etc	Buy at Auction	Planning Gain
Type of Finance:								
BTL personal	X							
BTL Limited Co	X							
BTL HMO	X							
Light refurb		X						
Commercial Mortgage	X					X		
Development finance				X	X	X		
Bridging			X	X	X	X	X	X
Auction Finance							X	
Crowdfunding			X	X	X	X		X

A general principle of lending to bear in mind is that rates vary according to the type (or level) of risk to the lender. Other factors affecting the availability of finance to **you** will include your experience as well as your creditworthiness. We will deal with your credit rating below, but first a word about mortgage advisors.

Mortgage Advisors

Many lenders nowadays, including some of the big lenders even for straightforward 'vanilla' buy-to-let, insist that you apply through an advisor or broker, who must either be on their panel or work through a third party who is.

You might wonder what the difference is between an Independent Financial Advisor (IFA) and a mortgage advisor or broker. Broadly, financial advice is split into three main areas:

1. General investment advice (this includes for example stockmarket-based investments);

2. Insurance and general financial protection;

3. Mortgage advice.

When you want to arrange a mortgage, the advisor must be qualified for number 3: mortgage advice. They may or may not also be qualified in one or both other areas. Those who give a broad range of advice tend to call themselves IFAs while the singly focused are simply mortgage advisors or brokers.

While good all-round financial advice is often useful, specialisation in mortgage advice can also be a good thing and there are some very creative and knowledgeable mortgage brokers. Some are landlords and property investors themselves who choose to work exclusively with other property investors in arranging the best finance. A list of some recommended advisors is included in the reference section at the end of this chapter.

Your Credit Rating

The most fundamental thing about getting credit is that you need to be creditworthy! It is worth having an idea of your credit rating. Make sure you value it and keep it *clean* by not missing any payments.

The first thing a lender will do is check your credit rating score, which gives an indication of how well you have managed credit in the past. The higher your score, the more likely any applications you make for credit will be accepted. The lower your score, the harder it will be for you to borrow.

A higher credit score will also enable you to qualify for some of the lowest interest rates available. With a lower score, even if you can get credit, you may be considered "sub-prime" and therefore a greater risk, so will only be eligible for lending at higher rates of interest.

The main three credit reference agencies which keep records of your credit rating are:

- Equifax (www.equifax.co.uk)

- Experian (www.experian.co.uk)

- Callcredit (www.callcredit.co.uk)

You can get a copy of your credit file from any of these agencies online for around £2, or for example from www.checkmyfile.com where you can see reports from all three, but the subscription cost after a 30-day free trial is £14.99 per month. Some banks and credit card providers also provide customers with free access to their credit report (including Barclaycard and Tesco Bank).

Assuming you are creditworthy and have the income level that may be required, you should be eligible for finance. Buy-to-let mortgages are the most common form of property finance – including variants for HMOs, limited companies and light refurbishment. You also need to factor in the new Prudential Regulation Authority (PRA) regulations.

Buy-to-Let Mortgages

Buy-to-let mortgages are among the cheapest form of borrowing (aside from home-owner mortgages), compared to any other form of lending to property investors or developers. They tend to be arranged on an interest only basis, making payments more affordable and the amount that can be borrowed greater, but they can be arranged on a capital repayment basis if required.

As you would expect, rates are more competitive for borrowers with a good credit rating and those with larger deposits, normally up to 75%, but there are some loans available up to 80 % loan-to-value. At lower loan-to-value ratios, for example if borrowing no more than 65 %, rates are often better.

Buy-to-let mortgages first came about in 1996, when a group of pioneering lenders recognised that changes in the law leading to the Assured Shorthold Tenancy (AST) agreement would make it easier for landlords to recover property from tenants when necessary, giving both landlords and lenders greater security over their assets.

As a result, lenders created products that enabled a mass market to develop, enabling ordinary people to buy properties to rent, having only to save a deposit and get a buy-to-let mortgage. Before that, buy-to-let was predominantly the preserve of wealthy self-financed landlords and commercial companies.

In 2015, the Council for Mortgage Lenders (CML) reported that lenders had advanced more than 1.7 million buy-to-let loans since they began monitoring the market in 1999, and that the buy-to-let market had doubled in size over the past 12 years. They also reported that buy-to-let mortgages now totalled over £200 billion.

Since 2015, tax and other changes such as increased stamp duty have begun to soften the growth of the buy-to-let market, as further discussed elsewhere. In 2017 the Prudential Regulation Authority (PRA), part of the Bank of England (BOE), began imposing rules on lenders to make sure borrowers do not overextend. The first set of new rules was aimed at applying stricter stress tests to borrowing.

PRA Interest Affordability Rules Introduced in January 2017

The Prudential Regulation Authority (PRA) introduced tougher stress test requirements that lenders had to apply to buy-to-let lending from January 2017. The new rules can make it harder to make the figures stack up on deals, so you may not be able to borrow as much as before.

The Bank of England is behind these new rules (and the PRA) and has stated that the clampdown is designed to protect borrowers from being overstretched, particularly in the event of any interest rate rises. Interest rates have recently risen from the all-time low of 0.25 % to 0.5 % and this represents the first interest rate rise for ten years. It does seem sensible to be cautious in our expectations for future interest rates, as they are not likely to go anywhere except up! However, it is widely expected that any increases will be minimal and slow to happen.

Under the new PRA rules, lenders must check that borrowers could afford their mortgage repayments if interest rates went up as high as 5.5%. (There are a few exceptions, such as on five-year fixed mortgages, or when remortgaging but not increasing the amount of borrowing.)

To give an example under the new rules, if a property is generating £1,000 per month in rent, then under the old rules using a 5% interest rate and 125% rental cover, you could borrow £192,000, but under the new rules the interest rate used must be 5.5% and rental coverage 145%, so the amount the landlord can borrow is now just £150,470.

Another way of looking at it is that if you want to borrow £150,000, the rent you would have had to receive would be £781 per month, but under the new rules the rent needs to be £997 per month. There are concerns that this is likely to push rents up further as landlords struggle to afford to buy.

How Much Can You Borrow?

The PRA formula introduced in 2017 requires the rent (the annual sum of monthly rent x 12) to be divided by 5.5% (the 'stress-test' interest rate) divided by 125% (the maximum borrowing levels relative to rent, given the interest rate applied). Given this formula, the table below shows maximum borrowings for various rent levels, but note that some lenders may apply stricter criteria such as requiring maximum borrowing at 145% rental coverage instead of 125%, which will lead to lower maximum borrowing.

Rent (per calendar month: pcm)	Maximum Borrowing at 125% rental cover
£400 pcm	£69,818
£500 pcm	£87,273
£600 pcm	£104,727
£700 pcm	£122,182
£800 pcm	£139,636
£900 pcm	£157.091
£1,000 pcm	£174,545
£1,200 pcm	£209,455

You can use the chart above to work out how much deposit you will need as well as seeing the maximum borrowing supported by various rents. For example, take an average-priced property at £235,000 with a rent of £1,200 pcm:

The usual maximum loan to value (LTV) requirement of 75% limits the mortgage to £176,250 while the rent supports borrowing of up to £209,455; so, the loan in this case is not limited by the new rules but by the 75% LTV requirement that was present before the new PRA rules came in.

But note that where the rental yield is relatively low, a product that allows up to 75% loan-to-value lending may be restricted by the rent level and may be further restricted by the new tougher PRA rules. For example, if you paid £235,000 for the property but the rental valuation was just £900 or even £1,000 per month, you would not be able to borrow the full 75% sum of £176,250.

Further PRA Rules Introduced in September 2017

The Prudential Regulatory Authority (PRA) claims that arrears rates increase as portfolio size grows and has introduced a new additional set of rules from September 2017. The new rules dictate that landlords with four or more (mortgaged) properties – 'portfolio landlords' – must meet new mortgage lending requirements and go through a separate and more stringent underwriting process. Each lender has *some* scope to create their own exact policy, but they are basically similar. Even if you just remortgage or buy one property, the lender is still obliged to go through this process. They need more staff, systems, paperwork and experience. Some as a result have even bowed out.

The PRA suggests buy-to-let lenders request the following:

- Business Plan

- Cash Flow Forecast

- Property Portfolio Schedule (/spreadsheet)

- SA302s and Tax Overviews from HMRC

- Bank Statements (usually 3 – 6 months)

- Assets and Liabilities Statement

- Tenancy Agreements

Lenders will not necessarily request all of these but could do. It may sound daunting, but to make it easier for themselves and their clients, many have produced templates, and some mortgage brokers may have generic templates to help their clients too. To be fair, larger portfolio landlords such as myself have been required to submit these additional items with any mortgage application for some time, but it now applies to all landlords with four or more properties.

Buy-to-Let Mortgages for a Limited Company

The question of whether to buy in a limited company structure is largely a matter of the tax implications and it is important to consider tax and finance together. Seek professional advice for your own circumstances and read the chapter on tax. There are also mortgage implications.

The phasing out of mortgage tax relief is encouraging more landlords to own their buy-to-let portfolios through a company rather than hold as a personal asset, which largely explains why limited companies now account for 76% of buy-to-let lending by volume, according to Mortgages for Business (see reference section), up from 63% in the first quarter of 2017.

Before the tax changes affecting mortgage interest, landlords often bought in their own names partly because there were more mortgage products available and at cheaper rates than for limited companies which was less mainstream. However, now that the demand for limited company mortgages has risen, the supply of such mortgages has risen and rates have fallen.

HMO Mortgages

If you wish to set up your property as a House in Multiple Occupation (HMO), you should ensure that you have the correct type of mortgage in place otherwise you could be in breach of the mortgage conditions. Mortgages for HMOs are reasonably plentiful, so this should not be a problem.

According to Mortgages for Business, in 2017:

> *"Around a quarter of all buy-to-let products (around 249 of 1,081 products) are available on HMO property (both licensed and multi-let) from around 15 different lenders – that's nearly half of all buy-to-let lenders. Most products are available on either a purchase or remortgage basis to both individual and limited company borrowers."*

HMO rates are generally higher than their vanilla buy-to-let counterparts, but many are reasonably priced.

To qualify for an HMO mortgage, it is not only the rent, the property, location and tenants that the lender will look at, but you. Many lenders prefer borrowers to have experience as a landlord before they will consider you for an HMO mortgage. Many lenders will want to know whether you intend to self-manage or use an agent for your HMO. They will also ask questions about how you intend to set up your HMO, for example the number of letting rooms, whether it will require a licence, the tenant type you will let to and so on.

Light Refurb Mortgages

Whatever the type of let, from single lets to HMOs, buy-to-let lenders normally require the property to be habitable and let within approximately 30 days of purchase.

To be considered habitable, the kitchen and bathroom must be usable and there must be no structural problems or serious damp issues. Most lenders will accept a few weeks of general redecoration may be required prior to letting but will not be willing to accept anything more that needs doing without at least some retention of funds, if they will lend at all.

A retention is when the lender withholds part of the mortgage until certain works have been completed on the property. We had this issue a couple of times. One example was when the valuer (a surveyor who looks at the property on behalf of the lender during your mortgage application) reported to the lender that he thought there was a chance of rot or infestation of the wooden porch. The lender put a retention on the mortgage of £3,000, withholding the amount until we could submit a full report on the matter after purchase and get any necessary work done. Once sorted, they released the £3,000 which was then added to the mortgage total.

While retentions may be available with ordinary buy-to-let mortgages where the property is habitable, it may otherwise be necessary to get a light refurbishment mortgage. Such products are aimed at properties that are unsuitable for letting at the time of purchase, possibly due to the lack of a working kitchen or bathroom.

As the name 'light refurbishment' suggests, such mortgages are not designed for heavy refurbishment works.

What is the difference between light and heavy refurbishment?

Light refurbishment can include any cosmetic improvements as well as the installation of a new kitchen or bathroom, re-plastering or even damp proofing.

Heavy refurbishment includes any major structural work, such as works that may require building regulations or planning permission.

If you are looking to finance anything other than a property that is habitable and ready to let within a few weeks, or suitable for a light refurbishment mortgage, you will not be able to use buy-to-let style mortgages, but will need other forms of finance, from bridging to development finance, and commercial mortgages or other financial instruments.

While the terms used can seem interchangeable and they are at times used loosely, in general:

- **Development finance** is mainly restricted to new-builds and significant conversion projects;

- **Bridging finance** may be used in a wider number of scenarios;

- **Commercial finance** is normally for commercial premises, but can be portfolio residential;

- **Other specialist types of finance**: there are many forms of finance that are less often used.

We will now look at development finance, bridging and commercial mortgages and other types of finance.

Development Finance

The term *development finance* is sometimes used loosely for any finance to do with developing property, but strictly speaking is mainly restricted to new-builds and significant conversion projects that are ready to commence as soon as the loan is granted.

Development finance is mostly available to experienced developers and for bigger projects, although a good business plan with realistic expenses can help present your case well to lenders. It tends to be available for 12-24 months, as it is for bigger projects that take longer to build out and sell on or refinance than say shorter bridging loan terms allow.

Interest rates may be assessed on each application individually, according to the strength of the proposition and the borrower, and could be from around 6% per annum.

The interest may be rolled up into the loan so there are no monthly payments, which is handy given that developments do not produce cash flow from rental income, unlike buy-to-let.

How much can you borrow?

For extensive projects and ground-up developments, the finance can cover both land purchase and building costs. For example, if a developer wants to buy a plot of land for £100,000 and spend another £500,000 building properties on it, a lender might finance 50% of the plot purchase and 70% of the build.

In this example that would mean the developer would only need £200,000 of their own money, rather than the total of £600,000 that the whole project costs – freeing up their personal capital for other projects, or unexpected expenses.

The loan amount will take into account the end value, namely the gross development value (GDV), up to a maximum normally of 60% loan to GDV, with a maximum of 75% of the total costs. Loans are normally structured so that the developer's contribution is used upfront, while the lender provides the majority of the subsequent build costs. Funds are usually available to be drawn down (released) in stages, upon an architect's or quantity surveyor's certification being produced.

It should be noted, however, that where the borrower has other unencumbered property which a loan could be secured against, they could borrow up to 100% of the property development costs.

The level of funding may also be increased if the planning consent is upgraded – for example, to allow for a greater number of homes to be built.

Property development loans are usually on an interest only basis, while the length of the loan (the term) may depend on the size and complexity of the project.

It is difficult to secure development finance without full planning consent being in place, so it is best that planning permission is gained before you seek such finance. Often developers may secure a potential deal with the use of option agreements (discussed in Chapter 2 on Sourcing) so that planning permission can be lined up before purchase. Developers may otherwise seek crowdfunding to support the costs involved in planning gain.

Bridging Finance

Bridging finance is one of the most flexible forms of property finance, but it is designed to be short-term and is quite expensive to use. Rates tend to be higher than development finance or any other type of finance.

While development finance is based on the Gross Development Value (GDV) ie the expected finished value of the development, bridging finance is based on the value of the land or property as it **is** at the time the loan is taken, not allowing for any uplift in value. It is very much designed to be short-term – like a bridge, getting you from here to there – to allow for works or planning permissions that will enable you to sell at a profit or move on to longer-term finance.

One of the advantages of bridging loans is that they can be arranged quickly, even in some cases as quickly as 24-48 hours, enabling you to secure a deal that might otherwise have got away.

The lender will take a first charge and will want to know your 'exit plan' for the end of the loan term.

What is an 'exit'?

An exit refers to your plans, which lenders will want to know, as to how you are going to repay the bridging loan at the end of the term, either by selling or moving on to a longer-term type of finance.

Some bridging loans may be 'closed loans' with a fixed exit date in place. This may be suitable where a clear exit is already lined up. Others may be 'open bridging loans' where there is no fixed end date but you will normally be given 'up to' a certain period, usually no more than 6 months to a year, to exit.

The interest rate can normally be rolled up until the loan is redeemed, which is useful for those without the required funds at the early stages to make interest payments.

Bridging loans can also sometimes be used in other situations where a short-term temporary loan is required, providing again that there is a clear 'exit' from the loan.

Auction Finance

Auctions can be a good way to get a property at a discounted price, if you get it right. There are lenders who specialise in auction finance, which is a variant of bridging. While some firms specialise in auction finance, others may offer a wider array of bridging products.

Given that you normally have only 28 days to complete on an auction purchase, bridging can be ideal. Many properties available at auction often need work too and may not be habitable, making them ineligible for buy-to-let mortgages until they are brought up to habitable standards.

There are some lenders who'll give you finance before you attend an auction, so you can arrive with an 'agreement in principle', though availability may be limited to experienced developers and landlords.

Commercial Mortgages

Commercial mortgages, as the name suggests, are most commonly used to provide mortgages for commercial property such as shops, offices and warehouses – or almost anything that is not residential property. They work in broadly the same way as residential mortgages, enabling you to spread the cost of the purchase over a number of years.

Commercial mortgages are available to a range of businesses, from sole traders to limited companies, and lenders will normally fund up to 75% of the purchase cost, similar to residential mortgages, with terms of up to 30 years. The affordability is normally determined by the profitability of the business and its ability to make the monthly payments.

The most straightforward scenario is where an existing business wants to take out a commercial mortgage to enable them to buy or refinance the premises where they operate their business already. It is possible to get a commercial mortgage for a new business although it is more challenging because there is a greater perceived risk to the lender. It could help if you have other security to offer the lender, such as another unencumbered property (one with no finance on it).

Commercial Mortgages for Buy-to-Let Portfolio Lending

Commercial mortgages can also be used to finance or refinance whole or part portfolios of buy-to-let properties onto one combined mortgage, and this variant, offered by commercial lenders, is often known as portfolio lending. Where this type of commercial mortgage differs from buy-to-let is a matter of scale, as it would only be available to more experienced landlords with bigger portfolios and will span several properties.

I had such a commercial mortgage for a few years across a few properties in my portfolio and the main reason for getting it was that lending became harder to find at the height of the financial crisis around 2009, but I wanted to carry on buying as I was confident of recovery in our area.

The finance was more expensive and on less favourable terms than the usual buy-to-let mortgage, but to me it was worth getting at the time. The terms of the mortgage allowed for only 10 years on interest only followed by 10 years on capital repayment terms. When I sold one of the properties, the lender required the cash realised from the sale to be used to further pay down the mortgage, which was limiting, but I had planned to pay it off within 10 years and ended up repaying the whole lot early anyway.

Other Types of Finance

We have now looked at all the most usual types of property finance, but there are many variations and hybrids. For example, while many bridging companies just do bridging and companies that offer 'development finance' usually just do that, there are a handful that have a foot in both camps. And while hardly any offer mortgages too, there are a couple that have recently added buy-to-let mortgages to their range. A select few mortgage lenders may also do some bridging as an aside, although this is quite rare.

If you are a landlord with any unencumbered properties (free of finance) in your portfolio, these could be used to secure lending. With enough equity free in your portfolio, you can get finance to buy more properties – allowing you to grow your portfolio without having to keep liquid cash.

This could be especially worthwhile if you are not sure when, how much or how often you might want funds in future. This is a route I am taking. I was stockpiling cash with a view to possible future development projects, but it's also important that I deleverage the portfolio, given the tax changes not allowing mortgage interest as an expense.

It is also possible to get "offset" mortgages which allow you to pay down the mortgage as and when funds allow, in which case you pay less interest accordingly – but the mortgage allows you to drawdown the funds when you need them too. Offset mortgages are not very common unfortunately, but would be very handy with the mortgage interest tax changes, so I'm sure they would be popular if more lenders offered them.

Another similar product in effect is a "revolving credit facility" but this is uncommon in property. Another less commonly found type in property is "mezzanine finance" which combines elements of debt finance and equity, secured against a property.

While it can seem like there is a whole complex world of property finance, I hope that this chapter has helped to make the subject a little clearer. I would always recommend that you speak to a professional advisor to get help and advice for the best type of finance for your current needs.

And remember, if nothing seems to quite fit, you could also consider crowdfunding – the alternative finance option, or joint venturing.

Crowdfunding

Crowdfunding was considered in Chapter 9 as it is a strategy in its own right; but I also mention it here to encourage you not to overlook it when considering your finance options. Crowdfunding can offer you flexibility, particularly if you find other finance routes are unavailable, and it can be relatively quick to arrange. It can also be fun.

Joint Ventures

Any type of deal could also be done as a joint venture with another investor, who may put in some or all of the cash. Note that if you do aim to set up a joint venture, you need to be aware of the FCA rules and ensure you are not breaking them. If you are hoping to attract investors, it is likely that crowdfunding will ensure you act compliantly instead, unless you are working with just one High Net Worth investor in a joint venture situation at a time, and they are fully aware of the risks and have entered the arrangement of their own volition – that is, not had the idea 'sold to them'.

Further Reading, Resources and References

Mortgage Advisors:

H D Consultants www.hdconsultants.net (independent financial advisors)

Lisa Orme of www.keys-mortgages.com (specialist mortgage advisor)

Kevin Wright of www.recycleyourcash.co.uk (mortgage advisor who also runs events for investors)

Bespoke Finance: www.bespoke-finance.info (mortgage and insurance advisors)

Mortgages for Business: www.mortgagesforbusiness.co.uk (property finance; many articles on website)

Funding Options: www.fundingoptions.com (for flexible business finance)

Credit reports:

- Equifax (www.equifax.co.uk)

- Experian (www.experian.co.uk)

- Callcredit (www.callcredit.co.uk)

- Check My File www.checkmyfile.com

Council of Mortgage Lenders Report: https://www.cml.org.uk/news/news-and-views/buy-to-let-the-past-is-no-guide-to-the-future

Landlord Today newsletter article on buy-to-let mortgages: https://www.landlordtoday.co.uk/breaking-news/2017/7/btl-mortgage-sector-continues-to-see-a-shift-towards-limited-company-lending

CHAPTER 11

TAX

"Every man is entitled if he can to order his affairs so as that the tax attaching under the appropriate Acts is less than it otherwise would be. If he succeeds in ordering them so as to secure this result, then, however unappreciative the Inland Revenue or his fellow taxpayers may be of his ingenuity, he cannot be compelled to pay an increased tax."

**Baron Thomas Tomlin in the
UK House of Lords, 1936**

Introduction

The first principle of taxation is, as the old quote above explains, that you are not under any obligation to pay more tax than you might if you can legitimately arrange your affairs to pay less tax. The Inland Revenue referred to is now of course known as Her Majesty's Revenue & Customs (HMRC).

The second principle is that there can be a fine line between the legitimate type of 'tax avoidance' referred to above, and 'tax evasion' which is not acceptable. Tax evasion occurs when you, either wittingly or unwittingly, order or declare your affairs so that tax which should have been paid is not.

It is crucial for property investors to understand this and plan as best as you can, with the help of your accountant and other tax professionals, to minimise tax legitimately, as getting it wrong can have dire consequences. It is also vital to be up-to-date, as every budget brings changes.

Current investors will understandably be most concerned about the tax changes of recent years that affect landlords, and which have forced many of us to adapt our businesses. These will be addressed in this chapter.

Tax is a subject of great concern for investors, since the changes announced by the then Chancellor George Osborne in the Summer Budget of 2015. However, everyone's circumstances are different, and some may be affected far less than others, while many will be able to adapt their business based on a clear understanding and good judgment of what they need to do.

CLARITY is the watchword when it comes to property tax. You need a clear understanding of how much tax YOU will have to pay and the extent to which YOU will be affected by changes, to guard against absorbing more negativity from the press and others than necessary. If you allow negativity to put you off without careful examination of the facts, then you will be missing out on property which is still the best investment for many in my opinion.

As landlords with a large portfolio of leveraged properties owned in our personal names, Dave and I are prime targets of the tax changes and have taken steps to adapt and change. However, despite thinking it's unfair and paying very high levels of tax, we make a lot of money and our business can very well survive the tax changes.

I do feel for the minority who find themselves trapped in a difficult or even impossible situation. However, most will be able to adapt and find ways to survive and that is what this book aims to help you do.

Of course, I am not a tax expert nor qualified to give advice, so any comments I make should be taken as my opinion only.

Let's start by looking at the basics. What taxes do property investors have to pay?

1. **Tax upon purchase**: Stamp duty is payable as soon as you buy property.

2. **Ongoing tax during ownership**: Either *Income tax* if you own property personally, or *Corporation tax* in a limited company. (We will also look at what expenses are allowed to be offset against tax. Most of the same expenses are allowed, except that mortgage interest is allowed for limited companies – BIG difference!)

3. **Tax upon sale**: Capital gains tax is payable when you sell investment property that you own personally, or corporation tax if it is owned in a limited company. You will pay income tax for individually owned property if you are a trader, ie it is a buy-to-sell project or development.

Those are the basics, but we also need to look at:

4. How tax is calculated now, under the new 'Section 24' (or 'Clause 24') rules.

5. Incorporation: what are the pros and cons of putting properties into a limited company to pay lower rates of tax?

6. Some activities, mainly service areas such as short-term lets, may attract VAT.

7. Estate planning and inheritance tax.

Whole volumes are written by tax experts and there are many nuances that can apply in individual cases. I can only give a rough outline of the relevant taxes. It is imperative that you seek tax advice for your own situation from your accountant or from a property tax specialist.

Stamp Duty Land Tax (SDLT)

When you buy any property over £125,000, you must pay stamp duty, officially called stamp duty land tax (SDLT), and when any purchase will result in you owning more than one property (from April 2016) you will have to pay a 3% surcharge on the stamp duty that's due.

Rather like income tax, stamp duty is charged in bands. Current rates are shown the table below:

Property (or lease premium or transfer value)	SDLT rate for first only property	Surcharge applies when you own more than one property
Up to £125,000	Zero	+ 3%
The next £125,000 (from £125,001 to £250,000)	2%	+ 3%
The next £675,000 (from £250,001 to £925,000)	5%	+ 3%
The next £575,000 (from £925,001 to £1.5 million)	10%	+ 3%
The remaining amount (above £1.5 million)	12%	+ 3%

For example, if you buy a house for £275,000, providing it is your ONLY home, the SDLT you owe is calculated as follows:

- 0% on the first £125,000 = £0

- 2% on the next £125,000 = £2,500

- 5% on the final £25,000 = £1,250

- Total SDLT = £3,750

From November 2017, first time buyers will pay NO stamp duty on the first £300,000 of a purchase price up to £500,000, a cut of up to £5,000.

Assuming you are buying an additional investment property, then all figures above are subject to an additional 3% surcharge, as shown in the table above.

If you buy several properties at one time, then you may be able to claim multiple dwelling relief; so instead of being charged as if it's one transaction that would otherwise attract higher rates (for example if total values = £1.52

million, you might think you'd pay at the rate of 12% + 3% ie 15%), multiple dwelling relief allows you to pay the rate of the average price. If each property is worth just £125,000, then you only pay at a rate of 2% + 3% = 5%. (But even if the individual properties were valued below £125,000, you would have to pay the minimum rate.)

For transactions with an effective date on and after 1st March 2018, the filing and payment window for SDLT is to be reduced from 30 days to 14 days.

Income Tax

Rental income derived from property owned in your personal name is subject to income tax at the tax rates shown below, assuming a standard personal tax allowance of £11,850 (tax year 2018/19):

Table 1: Income tax rates and bands

Band	Taxable income 2018/19 onwards	Tax Rate
Personal Allowance	Up to £11,850	0%
Basic rate	£11,851 to £46,350	20%
Higher rate	£46,351 to £150,000	40%
Additional rate	Over £150,000	45%

Note that the tax level is applied to income within each band. For the tax year starting 6th April 2018, any income up to £11,850 is tax free; any income that is between £11,851 and £46,350 is taxed at 20% and so on, regardless of whether your total income is over this threshold. However, you don't get the Personal Allowance on taxable income over £123,000. See gov.uk for more details.

What Expenses Can be Offset Against Tax?

Here is a list of ten main expenses that can be offset against tax:

1. Mortgage interest for companies or tax credit to 20% for individuals;

2. Repairs and maintenance;

3. Motor expenses;

4. Office costs;

5. Travel and subsistence;

6. Training and research (including books!);

7. Net cost of replacing furnishings (but no 'wear & tear', see below*);

8. Legal and professional fees;

9. Pre-trading expenditure including refurb, council tax** and utilities;

10. Rental losses.

*You used to be able to claim a 'wear & tear' allowance at a rate of 10% of rental income on furnished properties, but this has been abolished from the tax year started 6th April 2016. You can now claim instead only for the net cost of furniture replacement but not the ongoing wear and tear.

** In the November 2017 budget, it was announced that councils may now charge up to 200% on empty properties although this will generally only apply to properties that lay empty for two years or more.

VAT

VAT (Value Added Tax) is not payable on residential rental properties, so is not applicable in buy-to-let.

It is a tax charged on traders with sales above the VAT threshold (currently £85,000) who register for VAT and charge it on supplies of goods or services, which they then pay over to the HMRC. The standard rate of VAT is 20% although some things are charged at a reduced rate of 5% (including household fuel such as gas and electricity).

If you are not VAT registered, then you cannot reclaim VAT that you've paid, but traders who are registered can reclaim the VAT they've been charged by their suppliers, paying the net amount to HMRC.

The 'service elements' of short-term lets may be subject to VAT if your income goes over the VAT threshold, in which case you will need to register for VAT.

Capital Gains Tax

Capital gains tax (CGT) is payable when you sell an investment property that you own personally, or corporation tax if it is owned in a limited company. You will pay income tax for individually owned property if you are a trader, ie it is a buy-to-sell project or development.

In the budget of 2016, capital gains tax rates were decreased for the sale of assets other than property, but remained at higher levels in the case of property sales.

Table 2: Detailed example of capital expenses allowable against capital gains:

Purchase price at date of purchase:	£135,000.00
Sale price at date of sale:	£203,000.00
Gross Profit:	£68,000.00
All Capital Costs and Expenses:	£8,000.00
Net Profit:	**£60,000.00**
Description	**Amount**
On account with solicitor	£300.00
Mortgage Valuation fee	£354.00
Lender booking fee payable upfront	£250.00
Lender fees added to loan	£2,000.00
Stamp Duty	£1,350.00
Remainder of solicitor's fees at completion	£750.00
Pay seller's solicitor's fees	£750.00
Finder's fee	£766.00
Chaps Fee for sending completion money	£35.00
Total Purchase Costs:	**£6,555.00**
Description	**Amount**
Paid Zoom estate agent upfront for sale	£495.00
Solicitor's fees	£780.00
Apportionment of ground rent	£7.00
Service charge apportionment	£163.00
Total Sale Costs:	**£1,445.00**
All Costs at Purchase and Sale:	**£8,000.00**

As with income tax and SDLT, there is a lower limit to paying capital gains tax, an allowance. In the tax year 2018/19 you can make £11,700 profit before paying capital gains tax. (If you own property jointly, you each get the allowance before paying CGT, so if two people own it, then profits under £23,400 will not be taxed.)

As a basic rate taxpayer, you pay 18% capital gains tax on property sales over this allowance, while higher-rate and additional-rate taxpayers will pay 28%. The sale of your own home (or 'principle primary residence') does not incur CGT.

The tax is payable on the NET profit. Any 'capital' expenses, such as those incurred at the time of purchase (solicitor's fees and stamp duty) and at the point of sale (estate agents and solicitors), can be deducted from the difference between the purchase and sale price. Other capital expenses may be included too, such as the cost of a lease extension or remortgaging costs, or finder's fees.

The amount payable depends on several factors, such as whether it was owned by two or more people, each with a CGT allowance – assuming that was not used up by other sales in the same year. What income tax band each of the sellers fall into will affect them individually.

Let's assume the net profit of £60,000 above was on a rental property owned by two people with capital gains tax allowances not used up for the year.

Each person can take gains of £11,700 = total of £23,400; leaving capital gains tax to pay on the remainder. Let's further assume they are both higher-rate taxpayers and that the gain doesn't take them into the additional-rate bracket.

The capital gains tax due will be at 28%, after the total allowance of £23,400, on the remaining £36,600 = total CGT due of **£10,248;** assuming they owned the property 50/50, each is liable for half of the tax or £5,124.

To give another example, if the property had been owned by one person whose income is £30,000:

- This single seller has the personal CGT allowance of £11,700;

- The next £15,000 is taxed at a rate of 18% because it falls within their basic income tax bracket (up to £46,350) = CGT of £2,943 on this portion;

- The remaining £13,650 of net profit is taxed at 28% = £3,822;

- So the total CGT due in this case is **£6,765**.

Notice that the total CGT due is more in the second case (£12,164) than in the first case (£10,528), as even though the owner in the second case paid some of the gains at 18% while the pair in the first case paid it all at 28%, the couple could EACH make use of their capital gains tax allowance, whereas with only one owner this was limited to one allowance.

S24 – Tax Treatment of Mortgage Costs

In June 2015, the then Chancellor George Osborne, unveiled shocking tax changes that restricted landlords' ability to claim mortgage interest as an expense against tax.

Instead, finance costs are being restricted to the basic rate of income tax. This is being phased in from April 2017. These rules, announced in the Summer Budget 2015, are now contained in the Finance (No. 2) Act 2015 as amended by the Finance Bill 2016.

Investors often refer to these tax changes as "Section 24" or 'S24' in short, or sometimes as "Clause 24" and have attempted to fight the changes with support from professional landlords' associations, the Residential Landlords Association (RLA) and the National Landlords Association (NLA).

So higher-rate taxpayers who own property in their individual names can no longer offset all their mortgage interest costs against rental income. Instead of claiming mortgage interest as an expense, this will be replaced by a 20% tax credit only.

The change does not apply to property owned by a company, only to private individual landlords (as well as partnerships and limited liability partnerships). The change does not apply to furnished holiday lets, commercial or mixed-use (part commercial) properties.

The phasing in of the new rules restricts finance costs increasingly as set out below:

- 75% allowed for the tax year ended 5th April 2018

- 50% allowed for the tax year ended 5th April 2019

- 25% allowed for the tax year ended 5th April 2020

- 0% allowed from tax year commencing 6th April 2020

Experts have calculated that any higher-rate taxpayer landlord with mortgage costs above 75% of rental income may become loss-making. For additional-rate (45%) taxpayers, the threshold at which investment returns are wiped out by the tax is when mortgage costs reach 68% of rental income. It is therefore imperative that investors are NOT too highly leveraged under the new tax regime.

Some current basic-rate taxpayers will also be hit, because the change will push them into the higher-rate tax bracket. Very wealthy landlords who do not need mortgages will be untouched.

Some landlords, including myself, have reduced mortgage debt by selling some properties and using gains to pay down mortgages, while taking the opportunity to cull the worst performing properties, thus improving the overall quality of the portfolio.

You could also consider moving some properties into a limited company, particularly where there are no capital gains, but this could incur stamp duty costs.

Do not panic about the tax changes if you are affected, but give careful thought to what you can do to adapt, given your own circumstances. Incorporation for some could be the answer (see the next section).

Putting up rents is another thing which we, along with many landlords, have done as a direct result of the tax changes.

Landlords are trying many ways to limit the bad effects, including transferring properties to a spouse, making additional pension contributions and more. Whole books have been written about how to save property tax. Whether you read such volumes or not, you should always seek expert advice about your individual circumstances and future goals, as action you take to mitigate tax could have a knock-on effect that you may not have thought of.

The Daily Telegraph (see references) developed a buy-to-let tax calculator that gives an indication of how your profits will be affected by the new tax over the next five years. The example below is based on a hypothetical rental income of £100,000 a year, with 20% expenses and 65% loan-to-value (LTV) mortgages (on an assumed portfolio value of £2,000,000 with a gross yield of 5%) at an interest rate of 3%. (Minor changes in the budget of November 2017 to income tax thresholds and the Personal Allowance would vary these figures slightly.)

Buy-to-Let Tax Calculator Example

Description	Before changes	Transition year one: 75% interest relief	Transition year two: 50% interest relief	Transition year three: 25% interest relief	New Rules: no mortgage interest relief
Tax Year:	2016/17	2017/18	2018/19	2019/20	2020/21
Rental Income	£100,000	£100,000	£100,000	£100,000	£100,000
Expenses other than mortgage	£20,000	£20,000	£20,000	£20,000	£20,000
Mortgage Interest	£39,000	£39,000	£39,000	£39,000	£39,000
Profit before tax	£41,000	£41,000	£41,000	£41,000	£41,000
% interest relief	100%	75%	50%	25%	0%
Interest now taxable	£0	£9,750	£19,500	£29,350	£39,000
Taxable profit	£41,000	£50,750	£60,500	£70,250	£80,000
Tax chargeable	£6,000	£9,500	£13,400	£17,300	£21,200
Less 20% tax credit	£0	-£1,950	-£3,900	-£5,850	-£7,800
Tax due	£6,000	£7,550	£9,550	£11,450	£13,400
Net profit after tax	£35,000	£33,450	£31,500	£29,550	£27,600

(based on The Daily Telegraph Buy-to-Let Tax Calculator, reproduced)

Owning Properties in a Limited Company

A huge advantage for leveraged landlords of owning property in a limited company is that the new punitive S24 tax rules do not apply to properties owned in a company structure. The tax rate paid by companies is also lower than for higher-rate taxpayers.

UK Corporation Tax 2018/19:

Rate for profits up to £300,000	Rate for profits over £300,000
19%	30%

This section will take a further look at the pros and cons, but firstly, as many ask:

What About Moving Properties Into a Company?

Unless you incorporate your entire portfolio (see below), moving properties you already own individually into a limited company requires that you sell and the company buys, with all the usual implications of a purchase and sale, so you could be liable to pay:

- Stamp duty: the company buying the property will incur a potential stamp duty charge for any properties worth more than £125,000. This alone often makes the exercise prohibitively expensive, particularly given the 3% stamp duty surcharge.

- Capital gains tax: if there are any capital gains at the time of transfer, you personally as the seller are liable for this tax. You cannot just sell for a low price to the company, it has to be recorded at the open market value, and if you are getting a mortgage, the lender will get the property valued.

- Refinance costs: you also need to take into consideration that the mortgage you have on the property must be redeemed and a new mortgage obtained. This will likely incur application fees and the new mortgage may not be on such good rates or terms.

Incorporation of Whole Portfolios

Given the tax changes disallowing mortgage interest as an expense that only apply to individually owned property, many landlords are interested in exploring the possibility of incorporating their portfolio in a cost-effective manner.

There are pros and cons to having your properties in a limited company which will be looked at further in the next section, and there is more to consider than just the headline rate of tax.

It is possible to incorporate whole portfolios without changing the ownership, given the right conditions, thereby avoiding stamp duty and capital gains tax payments which can be rolled up, under Section 162 of the Taxation of Chargeable Gains Act (TCGA) 1992. Any profits or gains subsequently made by the company are assessed at the relevant rate of corporation tax – which is 20% and due to lower to 17% from April 2020. The company will also be able to continue, as companies can, to declare mortgage interest as an expense fully chargeable against tax.

This may seem like an obvious solution to the mortgage expense tax changes, but it may not be as straightforward as it might seem at first glance. There are complications such as whether or not your portfolio is currently run as a partnership, and experts do not always agree on when this condition is satisfied.

Some advisors say there is no need to tell your mortgage lenders (who are unlikely to agree to the arrangement) and that the cost of refinancing to lenders who are fully aware can be avoided by the use of a Beneficial Interest Company Trust. However, other advisors are uncomfortable with any arrangements that involve not telling your lenders.

I decided not to go down the path of incorporating my portfolio as it seemed to me and my accountant to carry the risk of HMRC refusing to accept it later, given they no longer give express upfront clearance on the matter. I also have mortgages on very good rates of interest that it would not be possible to match if I changed lenders.

Everyone's circumstances are different. I have good capital gains, am not too highly leveraged, have good mortgage interest rates and am in an area where selling is no problem. But some may have different circumstances that mean S24 is more calamitous and for whom incorporation may be their only hope of salvation. Or you may be somewhere in between, with your own different perspective.

As ever, make your own enquiries. I have put a couple of links at the end of the chapter to experts who you may wish to contact to discuss the matter further. Do your own due diligence.

The Pros and Cons of a Limited Company

While owning property within a limited company is in many ways good, there are a variety of factors to be borne in mind and you should as always seek professional advice given your circumstances and plans. To summarise, here's a list of pros and cons of using a limited company:

Pros:

1. Companies are not affected by the tax changes restricting mortgage interest as an expense.

2. The corporation tax rate, being 19% (and due to reduce to 17% from April 2020) on profits up to £300,000 per year (and 30% above that), is far less than paid by higher-rate taxpayers.

3. Corporation tax is also paid on gains at sale at the same rate of 19%, rather than the 28% *capital gains tax* paid by individual higher-rate taxpayers.

4. Children can be made shareholders, giving inheritance advantages (see next section for further details).

Cons:

1. Extracting profits from the company has tax implications that can counteract some of the advantages.

2. Unlike individuals, companies do not benefit from the Personal Allowance that individuals get – (which can be doubled for couples).

3. While some money can be taken out of a company tax free as dividends, this amount has been severely limited in recent years and is set to decrease further (see next section).

4. Companies have had the benefit of indexation relief upon sale which takes into account how long property has been owned so less tax is paid accordingly, but this is set to be abolished.

5. One of the key reasons that many landlords have not tended to buy in limited companies in the past has been that mortgage finance could be harder to obtain, but since the tax changes have increased demand,

this situation has improved with a lot more mortgage products available at competitive rates to companies than previously.

Dividends:

Since April 2016 the Dividend Tax Credit has been replaced by a new tax-free Dividend Allowance. This measure reduces the tax-free allowance for dividend income from £5,000 to £2,000.

You'll pay tax on any dividends you receive over £2,000 at the following rates:

- 7.5% on dividend income within the basic rate band

- 32.5% on dividend income within the higher rate band

- 38.1% on dividend income within the additional rate band

Estate Planning and Inheritance

The quality of our estate planning to provide for our families and other heirs will come to light upon our demise, and in that regard may be the final act by which we will be remembered. Was this, our final strategy, any good? I certainly hope so and will endeavour to do my best to make good plans. It is not easy as life – and death – are unpredictable and ever-changing, but with focus, care and action we can do our best to minimise the proportion of our wealth that is available for the government to snatch 40% of.

Without a will, your estate passes by default to your legal next of kin and in the event that none are found, the state (ie government) will get the lot. So, if you want to choose, make a will. Most of us would like to be in control of who our money gets passed on to, whether that be family, children if any, or anyone else, including charity, in whatever measure we choose.

When it comes to inheritance tax (IHT), each person has a nil rate band, currently £325,000, which they can pass on before inheritance tax becomes payable at 40%. Recent rules provide an extra nil rate band for your own home.

In April 2017 the residential nil rate band was introduced at £100,000, rising by £25,000 every year until 2020/21. So, in total, this residential nil rate band in addition to the standard nil rate band of £325,000 means that up to £500,000 per person can be passed on, or up to £1,000,000 free of inheritance tax, assuming much of a couple's wealth is tied up in their own home.

The residential nil rate band tapers away over £2 million, however, and will reduce by £1 for every £2 that the estate is worth more than the £2 million taper threshold.

If your estate exceeds or is likely to exceed the inheritance tax threshold, there are more ways to reduce your IHT liability, depending on your exact circumstances and aims. It is vital to seek professional advice from solicitors who specialise in IHT and estate planning.

I will not attempt to go into too much detail, as I am not an expert and any advice should be tailored to your needs. However, just to give you a brief idea, you should at least be aware of the following:

1. Gifts – Potentially exempt transfers (PETs)

2. Trusts – and Chargeable Lifetime Transfers

3. Shares – in a limited company (within the limits of lender requirements)

4. Business Property Relief

Gifts: Potentially Exempt Transfers (PETs)

When it comes to passing your wealth on, it is possible to give gifts during your lifetime of unlimited value, and these may be "potentially exempt transfers" (PETs) for inheritance tax purposes, meaning there will be no tax to pay on the gift so long as you survive seven years after it is made.

If you are thinking of gifting property, you cannot simply 'give the property away'; it must be valued as if sold at open market value for tax purposes. Upon the actual sale of the property, you will be liable for capital gains tax if any is due.

If you get property as a gift, you will not have to pay stamp duty (SDLT) as long as there is no outstanding mortgage on it. Only if you take over some or all of an existing mortgage will you have to pay SDLT if the value of the property exceeds the stamp duty threshold.

Note that you can only sell property to those over the age of 18, as minors under 18 cannot own property. If any children under the age of 18 receive income from property, the parents are still liable to pay the tax and the income is treated as theirs.

If you do not survive seven years after a gift is made, then tax will be calculated in accordance with the length of time you do survive after making the gift, as outlined below.

The 7-year rule

Potentially exempt transfers can be any amount so long as you survive seven years after making them.

If there is inheritance tax to pay, it will be charged at 40% including on gifts made in the three years before you die, on a sliding scale known as 'taper relief'.

Years between Gift and Death	Tax Paid
Less than 3	40%
3 to 4 years	32%
4 to 5 years	24%
5 to 6 years	16%
6 to 7 years	8%
7 or more years	0%

Taper relief on gifts made between 3-7 years before your death

Trusts – and Chargeable Lifetime Transfers

If you do not want to give gifts directly, you could make use of Trusts so that the benefit of assets is given without the asset ownership being transferred. This can serve to reduce your capital gains tax liability (as capital gains can be rolled up, or deferred) and the value of your estate, if planned carefully. Again, experienced professional advice is essential.

The use of a trust ensures that your estate goes to the people you want it to and that your partner cannot disinherit an unfavoured child for example, should you go first!

Trusts can also be useful to ring-fence assets. For example, if you leave money to your children but they later divorce, their ex-partner cannot lay claim to their money that is held in trust. Likewise, even if they are made bankrupt, the trust money remains protected.

You can gift up to £325,000 into trust in any seven-year period for it to be outside of your estate and then you have to wait for seven years before you can gift another £325,000 into trust. Each of a couple can put in this sum, so effectively it is doubled for a couple. If you put more than that into a trust within seven years, that amount becomes a 'Chargeable Lifetime Transfer' (CLT) which incurs an immediate 20% tax charge.

The benefits of trusts are certainly worthwhile, but note that trusts will have some set-up and admin costs and are taxed at the highest level of income taxation, currently 45%. There are various types of trust and you should seek professional guidance as to which is best to use in your circumstances.

If instead, properties or assets are simply bequeathed (passed on without being put into a trust), the net value forms part of the deceased's estate, in which case it is taxed at 40% above the nil rate threshold of £325,000. (If your properties are owned jointly, your combined nil rate band will be double.)

Some people think you can just gift your own home to your children and carry on living there, but it will still form part of your estate because you are still enjoying the benefit of the property by living there.

Shares – in a Limited Company

You may buy investment properties within a company and could make children or grandchildren, for example, shareholders of the company, even when they are minors who cannot own property. As shareholders, the value of their shares will rise in line with any increase in value of the properties. If a company property were sold and profits distributed, the children would pay tax on the sums they receive (or on dividends). Again, any income would be treated as the parents' if they are under 18.

It is a nice idea to make your children shareholders, but in practice we found our mortgage lender insisted we limit the children's shares, as they required the shareholding of the borrowers (myself and my husband) to be a minimum of 85%.

Business Property Relief

Business Property Relief (BPR) provides relief from inheritance tax on the transfer of relevant business assets at a rate of 50% or 100%. These could include (but seek advice as it depends on circumstances):

- A business or interest in a business. (Given the right type of business only, but this excludes a property portfolio or property development business.)

- Unquoted shares or securities which give control of an unquoted company

- Shares of companies quoted on the Alternative Investment Market (AIM)

- Quoted shares which give control of the company (50%)

- Land, buildings, machinery and plant of qualifying businesses (50%)

Some people advocate keeping all your properties until you die as a way of avoiding capital gains tax. It is tempting, as capital gains tax is wiped out upon death. But the pros and cons need careful consideration. If you put properties into a trust, capital gains arise but can be rolled up (ie not paid upfront). The idea of keeping your properties until you die is not as simple as it may seem.

For one thing, there is a limit to the age of a person that lenders are happy to lend to. Although this age limit has generally increased over recent years and it's possible you may not need to renew mortgages by the time their term expires (as you may have sold the property by then, or paid off the mortgage), it's another thing to consider whether you will still want a portfolio into old age, or will start to find the stress and hassle of it all too much. Even if fully managed, there will always be problems that come back to you as the owner.

Note that if your heirs do have a big tax bill but much of their inheritance is in the form of equity, they may have to sell some property to pay the tax bill. They may be given a limited time to do this, with HMRC demanding the tax be paid which could lead to a difficult and stressful situation. It is possible to get insurance to cover the estimated tax bill, but it can be quite expensive. Any such insurance should also be put in trust, to avoid it being itself liable to inheritance tax.

Finally, if you gift part of your estate to charity, this act of benevolence can reduce the inheritance tax rate payable on your estate from 40% to 36% providing you leave at least 10% of your estate to charity.

Further Reading, Resources and References

The website at www.gov.uk provides details including factsheets of all types of tax and allowances, as referenced in this chapter. As each link tends to be long and cumbersome and there are so many, not to mention there can be regular updates, I decided not to put the links to each individual topic.

Similarly, details of legislation can be found via www.legislation.gov.uk.

The Daily Telegraph Tax Calculator: http://www.telegraph.co.uk/property/buy/buy-to-let-calculator-how-will-new-tax-reduce-your-profit/

Residential Landlords' Association Landlords' Tax Guide: https://www.rla.org.uk/landlord/guides/tax-changes-affecting-residential-landlords-in-2016.shtml

There are many good books on tax and estate planning. Check the date of publication when choosing books on tax, as rules change constantly. Here are some suggestions:

Any book or publication by Tax Café. See www.taxcafe.co.uk

Book: *The Absolute Essence of Inheritance Tax Planning*, Steve Parnham, 2017

Contacts for whole portfolio incorporations: Mark Alexander, of: www.property118.com

Paul Bricknell, Partner, Tax and Probate, of: www.kuits.com.

CHAPTER 12

FINAL THOUGHTS

*"Develop clarity, energy, courage,
productivity and influence."*

~ Brendon Burchard

Adapt and Survive

The core message of this book is that it is essential to keep up with the ever-changing times and increasingly political environment in which your property business, or any business, exists. Legislation only ever increases, and politicians lean further away from supporting entrepreneurs. Hence escaping the lot of the masses becomes ever harder to achieve. You need the intelligence and cunning of a prisoner escaping from Colditz, it seems, to get anywhere in life these days!

So, will you make the great escape?

The fact is that when politicians latch on to what is making a lot of money, they want to milk the cash cow and put obstacles in the way of the masses. Your mission then, should you choose to accept it, is to find ways around the obstacles to stay one step ahead. You need to continually adapt to survive! You must be ready and willing to recognise the signs, spot the obstacles, navigate the minefields – AND spot the opportunities, the 'lucky breaks', the best strategies, the new horizons that could be your salvation.

This is not to say that you should run and hop at every rustle, like a scared rabbit. Stay calm and measured in your response, weigh the situation up carefully, stay focused on the business you have, but at the same time be flexible and *willing* to adapt if you need to. We are all hunted, we are all prey. We must be quick, when it's required, to survive. Once you start to build wealth, then you can begin to build yourself a financial fortress.

You do not have to do it all or try every strategy. Just be willing to look up now and then, and survey the landscape. But do only what is right for you, given your circumstances. Do not simply run in the direction that everyone else seems to be running in. It might not be the right direction for you. Start from where you are, with what you have and consider what is appropriate for **you**.

As the salutary lesson of the construction giant Carillion (who went bankrupt in January 2018) shows, you are never too big to fail. The saying comes to mind that *"you only find out who's been swimming naked when the tide goes out!"*, meaning that some people or businesses can appear successful but have all sorts of hidden flaws that eventually lead to their undoing. One of the lessons from Carillion is that a listed business can be too driven by how they *appear* to shareholders, or to others. Don't be like that. Build your business from the inside out. Be solid. Don't take on too much debt.

One wrong step can lead to a fall. So, watch your step – your every step. But keep going, and never, ever give up.

Keep Your Knowledge Current

It is essential to keep your knowledge current. In recent years there has been an unprecedented amount of new legislation in the property world that can have a massive impact – much of it in challenging ways. Given the current political climate, this is unlikely to ease up any time soon. It is therefore absolutely vital to keep up.

So how can you go about doing so? I suggest you watch out for budgets in particular, as that is when changes are often announced, and any other news concerning property. Aim to stay in touch in as many ways as you can find time for – and please do make time – both online and off.

Here are some suggestions:

- Online property forums such as at www.propertytribes.com and www.property118.com.

- Facebook has a number of very good groups, some with thousands of members, where various aspects of property and strategies are catered for and discussed.

- Two excellent property magazines that to my mind are essential are *Your Property Network* www.yourpropertynetwork.co.uk and *Property Investor News* www.property-investor-news.com.

- Online daily newsletters that I get include the inter-related www.landlordtoday.co.uk, www.propertyinvestortoday.co.uk, www.estateagenttoday.co.uk and www.lettingagenttoday.co.uk.

- Join at least one professional landlords' association, such as the National Landlords' Association (NLA) at www.landlords.org.uk or the Residential Landlords' Association (RLA) at www.rla.org.uk. Both run regular events and training courses as well as having helplines and a wealth of information to offer members.

- I try to get along to events when I can. I enjoy any events organised by the irreplaceable Brendan Quinn https://www.eventbrite.com/o/

brendan-quinn-events-720878069. I attend the National Development Summit which Brendan hosts once a year.

- I like to get along to John Corey's events in London when I can, which you can find via www.propertyfortress.com.

- Two of the most well-known property educators are Simon Zutshi of www.yourpropertyinvestorsnetwork.co.uk and Rob Moore who set up www.progressiveproperty.co.uk with business partner Mark Homer. Both have a national network of property networking events and also run mastermind programmes, as well as writing books and running courses.

- There are many more property networking events around the UK, including one for women hosted by Elsie Igbinadolor in London www.meetup.com/women-in-property-business-network.

There are so many ways to connect online today, and webinars or YouTube videos can be useful if you find it hard to get to events, but do not underestimate the power of connecting with other like-minded people in the real world. I love going online and also find it difficult to get along to events sometimes, but I can honestly say that meeting others through networking and belonging to groups has given a far greater boost to my levels of motivation than I believe is possible without actually meeting up with like-minded people. We are social creatures and programmed to respond more fully when we connect.

Mindset

Having a degree in psychology and a keen interest, I recognise my own tendency to focus or over-focus – for some people's taste – on the psychology of everything. I generally work at overcoming this tendency to psychologise or philosophise about life, the universe, property and everything!

I was surprised then when I read a book about inheritance tax planning where the author (a tax advisor) said he believes *"90% of the equation lies in the mindset"*, even in respect of inheritance tax planning! He meant that you will only take the necessary action to make great IHT arrangements if you have the right mindset about doing so – if you are determined and persistent.

To be fair, I think most people know that mindset is crucial to success and many would like to dwell on the matter more, but unfortunately there is simply not space in a book about property strategies that has so much information to impart.

The tax advisor was also making the point that the 'mechanics', if you like, of what needs to be done – the legislation that must be taken into account and the way your estate plans must be structured – should largely be left to your professional advisors; but you will only 'make it happen' if you have the right attitude. That is an important point about entrepreneurship: you do not need to know everything, you just need to know who to ask sometimes and be prepared to pay for good professional advice.

Take a look at my booklist in Appendix V and note the sheer number of books on psychology and mindset. Hopefully you will be inspired to read some of them. As you can see from the booklist, I am also keen on health and fitness, and longevity. I figured if the best way to build wealth is to own property assets and await massive capital growth, it seems prudent to live for as long as possible, in order to maximise the gains!

I have discovered in recent years that certain habits are known as "keystone habits", a term coined by Charles Duhigg in his book *The Power of Habit*. These are key habits that have the power to cause other good habits to develop and become aligned. For example, as a runner you are likely to eat better, sleep better and drop certain other habits like drinking too much – such bad habits tend to simply fall away as the *keystone habit* takes precedence.

Running has taught me a lot about self-discipline and mindset too. I have learnt to 'trust the science' – if you train regularly, you **will** get better, and this principle can be applied to other areas of life. You must also learn not to trust the *little voice* inside that says negative things like, *"I won't be able to run today"*. There have been many occasions when I had such thoughts, but I learned to ignore them and ran anyway!

I have also learned how motivating it is to get feedback: apps such as MapMyRun can help with that. Again, this principle can extend to other areas of life and business. What you focus on expands: what you measure tends to improve. You may not be interested in running, but I hope you find value in the principles of developing good keystone habits. It is also useful when it comes to your property goals to test and measure, track progress, and keep good records.

Often, when we are stuck, what stops us or holds us back can be about so much more than knowing the strategies to use. It is often our mindset that we need to examine and correct. For example:

- Decisiveness: Are you decisive and do you follow through?

- Support: Do you have the support of your family or business partners?

- Motivation: Do you really want it enough?

- Hidden attitudes: Examine your hidden attitudes to making money.

- Your values: Are they pulling you in other directions? For example, you think you want to make money but you're more focussed on caring for your family or on a hobby you love, which is all fine, but you need to recognise this.

- Clarity: You need to develop clarity on your own thoughts and most important goals.

Your mindset is the set of the sails that determine the direction of your life. Pay constant attention to your thoughts and beliefs, to ensure they are staying on course and are set for success.

Time and Productivity

Time is precious. It is your most valuable asset. You have to give some time to accomplish anything, and realistically, big accomplishments normally require a big commitment of time. You don't have to give it ALL up, but let it ADD up. If you give up just one or two hours a day to an important goal over a long enough period of time – be that weeks, months or years – you will be amazed what you can achieve. Be on a mission.

Everyone has the same amount of time but if you can be twice as productive, you can stretch time by doing more in the time available; whereas being slow or unproductive is like having less time. When I have a lot to do, I become more aware of how precious time is and speed up everything I do throughout the day, so I can fit it all in. Set yourself deadlines. A deadline focuses your efforts, so that you get more done.

We all know about setting smart goals (specific, measurable, attainable, relevant and timely) but remember to set goals that are time limited. Set up accountability by telling others what you are hoping to achieve too, and you will be motivated by not looking like an idiot if you don't achieve what you set out to do!

On the other hand, let go of the outcome if you can: have faith when you enter into a new project. Often as an entrepreneur, you have to put the work in way before you start to see any results or payback. It can be disconcerting, but trust the process and have the confidence of your convictions that the money will come. Too many people give up too soon.

You may know the fable of 'the acres of diamonds': the owner of a piece of land went off to seek his fortune after deciding there was nothing worth mining on his land, only to later find out – too late – that there were acres of diamonds in his own backyard. He just hadn't tried hard enough to find the treasure. I hope that this book helps you to find the treasure you seek and preferably as close to home as possible!

If you want to keep in touch, you can often find me posting on Property Tribes, joining in property groups on Facebook, or at events mostly in London.

Or you can write to me at angela@angelabryant.co.uk and let me know how things are working out for you after reading this book. Well, I hope!

If you have enjoyed the book, it would be much appreciated if you could consider leaving positive feedback on Amazon, as every little helps.

Further Reading, Resources and References

High Performance Habits, Brendon Burchard (Sept 2017)

Master Your Time, Master Your Life, Brian Tracy (Oct 2017)

See also the many links and references given in the second section of this chapter, under **Keeping your knowledge current.**

You may contact me at angela@angelabryant.co.uk.

APPENDIX I: Prop-Tech

The list below is just a selection of some of the new era of technology and apps that can help in property, sometimes known as prop-tech. Many of them are free, or at least have a free trial available. I have also included a couple of sites that offer virtual business addresses and virtual PAs.

There are always new technologies and apps coming to market which are worth a look. Many of these are based around the idea that it's good to be mobile: cloud-based apps that allow you to access your information from any device, and they also help you to share information with teams where you may work with others remotely. While not exhaustive, I hope the list includes some of your current or future favourites:

Airtable: www.airtable.com. Airtable *makes it easy to organise stuff, people, ideas and anything else you can imagine with your team.* Ryan described Airtable as *"like a spreadsheet on steroids".*

All Day PA: www.alldaypa.com. Offers 24/7 telephone answering service.

Arthur Property Management: www.arthuronline.co.uk. Property management software with a suite of apps that connects you with tenants, agents, owners, contractors and accountants.

Asana: www.asana.com. Asana promises to be *the easiest way to get teams to track their work – and get results.* Track projects from start to finish, make responsibilities and next steps clear.

Base Point: www.basepoint.co.uk. Offers a virtual office address.

BillHub: www.billhub.io. Bill Hub says it is *the simple, more secure way to send, spend and manage your money between housemates.* It can also help to find the best deals on utilities.

Citibase: www.citbase.com. Also offers a virtual office address.

Blogger: www.blogger.com. You can set up your own property blog (or blog on any subject) easily and free at Google's Blogger. It allows multi-user blogs with time-stamped entries.

Fiverr: www.fiverr.com. Fiverr is a marketplace where interested people competitively quote for jobs you need doing. Useful for help with website design and graphics, writing projects, music or voice-overs, programming, tech, and more.

Fixflo: www.fixflo.com. Provides a system for reporting and managing property repairs and maintenance. Most helpful for agents or landlords with larger portfolios, to be cost-effective.

Go Cardless: www.gocardless.com. Enables organisations to take card payments and set up direct debits simply and electronically. Ability to integrate with your existing accounting software such as QuickBooks or Sage.

Google Drive: www.google.com/drive. Google Drive is a cloud storage and file management programme which allows you to sync and upload files from your desktop, and lets you access your stuff on every computer and mobile device.

Hello Sign: www.hellosign.com. Allows electronic signature, useful when contracts need to be signed remotely without delay.

Homeit: www.homeit.io/en. System for keyless entry to short-term lets and Airbnb lets, holiday homes (even overseas in certain counties), etc.

Inbox by Google: www.inbox.google.com. Aims to improve email productivity and organisation. It can gather emails of the same topic together, highlights key details from messages, and has reminders, assists, and snooze functionality. It seems similar to Outlook, but more mobile.

Land Insight: www.landinsight.io. Site sourcing and deal management made simple. *Acquire off-market opportunities using game-changing technology.* (More on this in Development chapter.)

Live Home 3D: www.livehome3d.com. This interior design software can be used with Windows 10, to *assist both homeowners planning some home renovations and interior design professionals visualizing their projects.*

Magic Plan: www.magic-plan.com. For developers. Create floorplans. Estimate materials and costs. Order your materials.

MessageBird: www.messagebird.com. Communication software that enables you to use text, voice, chat and video over multiple channels.

No Agent: www.noagent.co.uk. Paid for service. You choose the extent to which No Agent fully manages. Add-ons can include all stages of the lettings process or just some.

People Per Hour: www.peopleperhour.com. Hire freelance or virtual assistants and other skilled roles.

Podio: www.podio.com. Includes a CRM (customer relationship management) package and offers *tighter collaboration for greater durability: clearly defined roles and a custom tool fitted to how your team works best will help improve delivery time, effectiveness and relationships.*

Slack: www.slack.com. Slack is a system that *unifies your entire team's communications, making your workflow flow a lot better.* It can be especially useful for teams that may not physically work from the same location. Use for sharing photos, receipts, etc. You can do video calls from there too.

SnapInspect: www.snapinspect.com. For inventories and property inspections, SnapInspect *lets you inspect properties, create beautiful reports and deliver them using your smartphone or tablet.*

Spareroom: www.spareroom.co.uk. Advertise rooms to let in shared housing, HMOs.

Trello: www.trello.com. Trello *lets you work more collaboratively and get more done.* Trello's boards, lists and cards enable you to organise and prioritise your projects in a fun, flexible and rewarding way.

Xero: www.xero.com/uk. Accounting software that claims to *help small businesses to thrive.* Helps with bookkeeping and can reconcile with your bank account.

APPENDIX II: Telephone Questionnaire

For Quick Sale Property Leads

Note that this was the questionnaire I used when calling back clients who had already made initial contact with the call centre at A Quick Sale and left their details, after it was established that they want to engage in the process. If it is the first contact from your marketing, you need to have that initial conversation first to make sure they understand your offer will not be at the 'retail' value but that you buy at a discount in return for offering a quick sale to solve their property problems.

Adapt the Telephone Questionnaire to suit your style and purposes, as you wish. (For example, if you have a rent-to-rent lead or wish to discuss an Option Agreement, the questions will vary.)

General Information	
Client Name, Address and Postcode	
Where did you hear about us? (to test your ads if more than one) Was that the first time you'd heard of us? (again, to 'test & measure') How much do you know about how we work? (Here you might see if they realise you buy "at trade prices" – ie at a discount.)	
What type of property do you have there? (You will ask for further details below)	
What do you think is the estimated open market value of your property? Why do you think that? (Ask sensitively, as they may be sensitive about it. Many over-estimate; say that you need to 'do due diligence' before you take things further.)	

Bear in mind that if it's not your target type of property or area, it may suit someone else you could pass the deal to. If it's wildly unsuitable – such as a very expensive house that won't stack for buy-to-let – you may just gently let them know that.	
Client Situation	
What is your main reason for wanting to sell quickly at this time?	
Try and ask more questions about their circumstances to dig a little deeper into their situation if they are ok with it. Some people love to tell all, others want to stick to business matters only.	
...... ANY OTHER REASONS?	
Property Information	**Some people get irritated by too many questions, so try to judge it... you don't need to ask all**
Confirm type of property, eg mid/end-terrace?	
Number of bedrooms? Doubles? Singles?	
Number of Receptions?	
Conservatory?	
GCH?	
Double Glazing?	
Age of kitchen and bathroom?	Kitchen = years Bathroom = years
Garage?	
Driveway? How many cars?	
Garden? Sheds?	
Conversions/Extensions? (If more beds – how many beds were there originally?)	
Cellars?	

When was the property built?	
Construction – Brick with slate/tile roof?	
If concrete or other non-standard construction, what specific type?	
Property / Client State	
How would you describe the **overall condition** on a scale of 1 (poor) to 10 (excellent)	
Issues? –Subsidence, damp, flooding?	
Environment – noise – roads, rail, etc	
Ex Council?	
Freehold / Leasehold?	
Time left on lease?	
Who lives there – adults over 18?	
What is the rent – ask only if it's currently an investment property?	
Is there anyone else on the title?	
If so, do they agree with the sale?	
Month and year bought?	
These finance questions are VERY IMPORTANT, as there's no deal if they have not enough equity; or partner doesn't agree!! Price paid for the property?	
Mortgage? Lender? How long for?	
Outstanding mortgage amount?	
Other secured loans?	Amount: (original/outstanding?) Since:
How much is your monthly mortgage? How much are other secured loan repayments?	
Any arrears?	

ONLY IF THEY SAY ARREARS, ASK: **Are you being threatened by your** **mortgage lender with repossession?**	
ONLY IF THEY SAY YES TO REPO: **What stage has it got to with the** **repossession threats?**	
Any Early Redemption Penalties (ERPs)?	
Outstanding amount include Arrears & ERPs?	
Total outstanding of Secured Debt (mortgage plus secured loans)?	
Any other debts you need/want to clear with the proceeds from the sale?	
If a **flat**, how much is ground rent?	
If a **flat**, how much are service charges?	£
Name of management company?	
If a **flat**, how many in block? Where's yours? Floor number of 'x' number of floors. At front/back of block? etc]	
If **flat above commercial** – what type of commercial premises?	
Retirement flat?	
Valuation	
Market value?	
How did you arrive at this valuation?	
Listed with estate agent? Name?	
How long?	
Have you had any viewings? Interest?	Offers:
Any offers? If so, how much? Why did it fall through?	Viewings:
Conclusion	
How time sensitive would you say this **is? (...do you really need quick sale?)**	
What is the best time for me to call you? (They may work and prefer an early evening call, for example.)	

Do you have a mobile number?	
What I will do now ("I will value the property", ie you will do your due diligence.)	
When I will next contact you… be clear and reliable.	
My contact details are: phone (optional, email).	**07xxx xxxxxx anytime** (leave a voicemail if necessary)

APPENDIX III: Interviewee Questionnaires

I sent out questionnaires to a few of the contributors for the book which I include here as completed by Ryan Carruthers (mentioned in Chapter 1: Strategic Planning), Glenn Ackroyd (see Chapter 7: Property Lettings and Estate Agents) and Davin Poonwassie (see Chapter 9: Crowdfunding).

Ryan Carruthers of Venture Property Lincoln

Ryan is a young investor who was mentioned in Chapter 1: Strategic Planning. He is very tech savvy and generally a rising star in my opinion. Ryan has got together with Kim Stones who is a mature and experienced investor with a lot of experience of HMO investing, as well as rent-to-rent. They now focus on development as well as HMOs. I invested in a crowdfunding deal they brought to market via Simple Crowdfunding recently.

Here are Ryan's responses to the questionnaire I sent out:

> **What did you do before property?**

Worked in Dad's company, owned a couple of Betfair Trading websites – Pro trading on Betfair.

> **What attracted you to property initially?**

I wanted to have something longer term. I was trading on Betfair, a competitor offered me a large sum of money for my business, I thought I would buy a single let for cash and then it would produce me £500 PCM and that would be a good start to build a small portfolio to go alongside my trading. Then I got bitten by the property bug and loved the deal making and the systems and everything!

> **How would you describe what you do for readers? What is your main strategy or focus?**

I use technology to manage every aspect of our business, which is a mixture of property development, HMO (professionals and students) and to find our deals for development. I have built a detailed tech system using Slack and my team to pretty much automate the running of the portfolio which allows me to do what I do best, find deals!

The main focus is now on development, and I spend a lot of time networking and finding deals in my local area of Lincoln.

> ### Is there scope for passive investors to get involved in this strategy?

Not really passive. I have some investors who work alongside us, and mainly they provide the funds while I do everything else.

> ### How much money would people need to do what you do? How much training?

Training would be minimal. I have spent a lot of time networking with people who do what I wanted to do and they helped me, teaching me what they do and taking me under their wing – mentors are so vital in my opinion.

Money wise, it doesn't have to be a lot but if you have no money you need to alter your expectations – people won't always give you the lion's share of the profits until you have a track record. So if you have limited money focus more on building the CV for profitable projects even if you have sourced the deal, ask to be involved in the project for free to get your CV strong – then you will be able to command a chunk of the profit in deals to come, plus learn about the next stage of the development.

> ### What do you see as the main risks in property today, or what risks are you facing?

PRA – it is getting a lot longer to get a mortgage, which can cause a deal to fall out of bed. With the right set-up though it shouldn't be too much of an issue to acquire the properties, but it will be more work getting the mortgage, business plans and cash flow forecasts.

➢ **What steps if any are you taking to ensure a good future for your portfolio, especially considering the tax changes?**

My plan is to pay down the mortgages on my portfolio, I will sell, sell, sell and keep a couple of big ones like the George & Dragon, but with no mortgage.

➢ **People often ask about TIME: How much time did you put in at the beginning, to get started? How much skill did you have?**

I had a bit of time at the start as I outsourced a lot of my other tasks in my other businesses, so I could spend time building the business and meeting people – I hand delivered all my original leaflets as well – every week for months!

➢ **Regarding scaling up – do you have staff now, or would you like to in future?**

I have a VA in the Philippines, a bookkeeper again in the Philippines and a self-employed cleaner and viewer who does a lot of the move-ins and viewings.

➢ **How ambitious are you? What motivates you?**

Good question. Very very ambitious. I want to be successful and create lasting legacies in the buildings I create. What motivates me is enjoyment, I am totally happy with my life because of the freedom that this business helps to provide me with and that motivates me to continue.

➢ **Do you combine what you do with other property strategies?**

Nope.

➢ **How well would you say your property strategy fits with other strategies and do you use a combination of strategies?**

I don't, we have a mix of HMOs and development which works well because of the tech systems that I have created that make it easier to manage.

> ➤ **What would be your advice to others on combining or adding on strategies?**

I would say initially pick one and go all the way you are physically able to, give it your full focus – when you have done this then look at adding in others, but keep management systems in place to monitor.

> ➤ **Can people use your services? Do you offer training, coaching or mentoring?**

I have a free Slack group (www.realestateslackers.com) and a podcast www.venturepropertylincoln.co.uk/podcast. I don't mentor or offer training.

> ➤ **What would be your top tips for readers: what are the most important things they need to know?**

It doesn't matter what strategy you do, just pick one that works for you. Be honest with yourself, there are so many ways to profit in property, so don't just pick a strategy because its cash flows are the best if you aren't going to be able to hack it. Also get professional advice for whichever path you choose – I was at first not happy, not wanting to spend £5,000 on a planning consultant but they know more about planning law then I ever will It's a cost to the business and will help you not only scale but get better deals.

> ➤ **Who inspires you? Are you into self-development? What writers or speakers do you like?**

I love Ray Lewis – he is a very motivational man. I read a lot of different business books, Tim Ferris, James Schramko.

> ➤ **If readers want to get in touch with you, where can they do that?**

ryan@venturepropertylincoln.co.uk

Instagram/ryancarruthers919

www.venturepropertylincoln.co.uk

Glenn Ackroyd, founder of EweMove.com

Glenn Ackroyd, mentioned in Chapter 7: Lettings and Estate Agents, and elsewhere in the book, is one of the founding directors, along with business partner David Laycock, of www.EweMove.com, a franchise company offering property management and estate agency. I first met Glenn when he was a director of A Quick Sale (mentioned in Chapter 2, on Sourcing) where I was a franchisee.

I always remember Glenn saying you should test and measure everything in marketing, and be very good at making use of technology in business too, as well as managing staff.

Here are Glenn's responses to the questionnaire I sent out:

> ### What did you do before property?

I got a job as a debt recovery manager for a firm of solicitors in Halifax. I then went on to qualify to become a 'Legal Executive', which is a poor man's lawyer. Working for a small firm, you get to do bits of everything, but I was attracted to Landlord & Tenant law.

> ### What attracted you to property initially?

My simple view was that if I could acquire five houses while working, it would replace my current income and I could retire.

Unfortunately, I became an addict, and my house buying got out of control. I'd bought three, and then I came across an opportunity to join A Quick Sale when it was just starting out.

> ### You were also a director of A Quick Sale before EweMove weren't you – so how did that come about? [Mention your portfolio as you choose too.]

In 2004, I wanted to buy more houses, but there had already been a big hike in prices, so I was worried that there might be a correction. I figured that if I bought 'Below Market Value' it would help to buffer me from the risk. At the time there was a brilliant website called SingingPig.com with contributors like Lisa Orme sharing great knowledge.

I saw a post by Richard Watters who founded A Quick Sale and we met and I joined on the spot. Shortly after he offered me a role as a Director with a shareholding in the business, and I left my legal job after 13 years.

I owe a lot to Richard because he taught me so much which provided the foundation for my later success.

➢ What led you to set up EweMove?

Necessity is the mother of all invention. After the credit crunch, I hung on by the skin of my teeth and threw everything into avoiding bankruptcy. That meant being much more efficient at managing my portfolio.

During my time at A Quick Sale, I met David Laycock who was a franchisee. He had a background in banking and was brilliant at systems, IT and financial controls. Between us, we set up a cloud-based solution to manage our large portfolios and that expanded into looking after other people's properties.

The business grew, and we decided that to scale, we needed to franchise our operation.

➢ What led you to sell EweMove and what are you looking to do next, if anything?

A sale to a PLC meant that the business had a solid foundation with enormous backing to enable it to grow. Until that point, it was entirely self-funded, with all profits re-invested for growth. We never took a wage or dividend, although I'd sneak a chocolate Hobnob when nobody was looking!

But aside from the business case, in 2008 I was on cloud nine thinking I'd 'made it'. Following the credit crunch, I was facing bankruptcy. This period of my life was horrible and I never wanted to return there. So receiving a sum of money that enables me to look after my family indefinitely was something I couldn't turn down.

➢ **EweMove is still going, under new management, isn't it: so how can people get involved in becoming a franchisee, or would you recommend it?! What sort of person would it suit?**

People can find out about joining EweMove by visiting EweFranchise.com. They should get a franchise pack and turn up to a Discovery Event to see if it's for them. It certainly suits current estate agents who want to free themselves from office and staff overheads and keep the lion's share of their profit.

But the truth is, you don't need any estate agency experience. Just great people skills, organisation and a willingness to do whatever it takes to provide the best customer service.

➢ **Would you say there's any scope for investors who want to be a bit more passive, to get involved in this strategy – as a franchisee? Or just someone using the services (like me!)?**

There is no such thing as being a passive franchisee! It requires a great system combined with hard work. There's a correlation between low effort and low risk, which means that most passive investments have low returns.

➢ **How much money would people need to get involved? How much training?**

The fee for an estate agent to join is as little as £1,995 + VAT. And the VAT is recoverable. You do need working capital. But with bank funding readily available, with £15k, you'll have enough to set up a great business.

The training is never ending! The onboarding takes place in the first week, but there are monthly training days, a video vault, webinars and Business Development Managers. We put a lot of focus on building a robust training programme.

➢ **What do you see as the main risks in property today, or what risks are you facing with your portfolio?**

The government!

It's impossible to plan when the goal posts are constantly being moved. Tenants now account for 1 in 5 households and are a big voting block.

So opportunist politicians offer endless waves of ill-conceived election bribes to win their favour. The result is a full-scale attack on landlords who are now beginning to exit from the marketplace.

The Council of Mortgage Lenders reported that a year after the introduction of the 3% additional stamp duty levy on second homes and Section 24 tax changes, landlord buy-to-let mortgages were down 50% year on year. With property investors selling, the rental stock will deplete very quickly, and we know that governments are useless when it comes to providing adequate social housing.

Corbyn has suggested that he'll bring in rent controls. While he might not win the next election, the Tories are desperate to appeal to the younger generation for votes. It's not inconceivable that they could even adopt this strategy. History tells us that this would lead to a mass exodus by landlords.

> **What steps if any are you taking to ensure a healthy future for your portfolio, especially in light of the tax changes?**

I've been buying property for cash in Limited Company Trusts for my children. I sell a couple of houses each year to maximise my Capital Gains Allowances and reduce mortgage debt.

I'm currently looking at moving into commercial property and serviced apartments. They have much better treatment on stamp duty and you can take advantage of capital allowances. Section 24 doesn't apply to limited companies.

> **People often ask about TIME: How much time did you put in at the beginning, to get started (in EweMove for example)? How much skill as well (you and David are good at tech stuff, organising, leading)?**

You need to do whatever it takes, which does involve time. I would do six 12-hour days a week typically. But I never saw it as work because I loved it (most of the time!). But working hard is not the critical element. You need a great product or service, great people and to inspire a brilliant team.

That's what we had at EweMove. David Laycock is incredible at automating systems and our renegade franchisees that came on board in the early days and backed our vision were amazing.

> ➢ **You of course had staff, which enabled you to scale up and I'm sure you recognised the importance of that. Do you have staff now, or would you like to in future ventures?**

We have some amazing 'A player' team members who remain personal friends. We owe so much to them for sticking with us and believing in us when the majority of people in the industry didn't.

David and I are currently 'between jobs' so we have no current business ventures. We plan to start a new scale venture, but we also like the idea of using third-party suppliers as partners rather than taking on hoards of staff.

If we did recruit, it would only be a handful of people with incredible talent. I hate writing birthday cards.

> ➢ **How ambitious are you now? What keeps you going?**

I'm not materialist ambitious. Even after the sale, I've not gone out and bought any of the stupid rich-kid toys that you'd imagine doing if you win the lottery.

I do like disruption. With EweMove, we didn't set out to be the biggest, but the best. I was so proud when our franchisees were rated by their customers as the UK's Most Trusted Estate Agent on Trustpilot.

I'm driven by a desire not to vegetate. I heard someone once say that you should always have more goals than memories.

Some of my current ones are helping my children succeed in life, running 10K in under 50 minutes, getting under 13 stone, setting up another exciting business and stopping my cat from bringing live mice into the house.

> **Do you combine what you do with other property strategies?**

Because my sole focus for the last few years has been on EweMove, I've not had much time to focus on my portfolio. Now that my day is freed up, I'm looking at other opportunities that may exist within property. That's led me to look at property development, commercial conversions and serviced accommodation.

I'm currently building three luxury homes which will take my total house builds to seven. I'm not quite David Wilson, but it's a modest start.

> **How well would you say your property strategy fits with other strategies and do you use a combination of strategies?**

I do use a mix of strategies, only because certain solutions work for some properties and not others. It's also good to try new things. You don't know what you don't know, so I'm always looking to expand my knowledge and keep boredom from the door.

> **What would be your advice to others on combining or adding on strategies to this one?**

You need to be careful. If you're always looking at multiple strategies to determine the best one, there's a risk you'll do none of them well. Do what you feel most comfortable with first and once you've mastered that, look to bring other complementary aspects into your business.

> **Can people use your services in this area? Do you offer training, coaching or mentoring?**

I don't like training or mentoring. I don't like being responsible for other people when I can't control what they do. And it restricts my time to do what I want to do.

I do help friends and people I come across with my highly opinionated business and marketing advice! My family hate me for it. I can be in a shop or restaurant, and I'll see something wrong and make a point of offering my constructive advice to the bemused owners.

➢ **What would be your top tips for readers: what are the most important things they need to know about property management and estate agency?**

For me, the key to good asset management is finding and keeping good quality tenants. That starts with providing quality, clean property in good repair. If you have a poor property, you'll only get tenants who'll accept your poor standards.

Vetting tenants is key. No tenant is better than a bad one. We visit them in their own home before signing and get homeowner guarantors.

And once they're in, deal with repairs quickly. So many landlords see tenants as irritants. They are customers. Imagine going on holiday and arriving at your hotel room, and the towels are dirty, or the TV doesn't work, and it takes three days to repair. You'd be livid. Many landlords expect tenants to be happy with unclean homes or leave them waiting days or even weeks for repairs.

It's a service business, and if you treat your customers well, they're more likely to pay a higher rent, on time and stay longer.

The other essential for any business, but particularly property, is to have good systems and processes. Jobs should be broken down in written form with easy-to-follow checklists.

Automate anything that can be done. This will improve efficiency and ensures a consistent level of service.

➢ **What are your thoughts about property taxation?**

It's important that you get good tax advice. I'd urge any landlord to sign up to the newsletters from Property118.com because Mark Alexander is the smartest person I know when it comes to setting up your property business efficiently to minimise your tax liability.

A good accountant and financial advisor are essential when you start to build wealth. I've been able to use the tax incentives to minimise my tax by paying into pensions.

Because I own houses jointly with my wife, we get double the benefits from Capital Gains Tax on sale.

Serviced apartments are attractive because you can claim between 20-40% of the properties' value to offset against income tax. So a £100k house may have up to £40k of capital allowances. This is offset against income tax. Only 4% of people use their Capital Allowances because they don't know about them.

I've lost so much money through ignorance, so never skimp on paying for good advisors.

> **Who inspires you? Are you into self-development? What writers or speakers do you like?**

I like self-development, but I'm not into reading books or following gurus. I love marketing. I'm fascinated with the concept of getting a product or service and dramatically increasing sales by using original copy and smart marketing techniques.

> **If readers want to get in touch with you, where can they do that?**

mrglennackroyd@gmail.com

Davin Poonwassie of Simple Crowdfunding

Davin Poonwassie, mentioned in Chapter 9: Crowdfunding, describes himself as a property and fintech entrepreneur who runs the growing crowdfunding site Simple Crowdfunding along with his wife Atuksha. The site is licenced for peer-to-peer or debt-based lending, equity-based investments and IFISA's too, all as discussed further in Chapter 9.

Davin was first introduced to crowdfunding in early 2013 when he spotted the opportunity that crowdfunding brings. At the end of 2013, Simple Backing – his first property crowdfunding platform focussed on peer-to-peer lending – was born. After speaking to customers, Davin soon realised that there was also a need to provide an equity option, thus Simple Equity was formed. With a background in data, databases and information technology, Davin is well suited to this marketplace.

Outside of crowdfunding, Davin is a business and property coach, helping others achieve their goals and aspirations. Davin is also a keen property investor, investing in parts of the UK and France.

Here are Davin's responses to the questionnaire I sent out:

➢ What did you do before property?

I was in IT as a DBA, designing and building solutions for local and global clients.

➢ What attracted you to property initially?

The creativity, challenge and independence – corporate life was not for me.

➢ How would you describe what you do for readers? / What is your main strategy?

This could be a long answer! The short version is we are a fully authorised and regulated platform providing a P2P, Equity and IFISA marketplace for property-related fund raisers and investors.

➢ Is there scope for passive investors to get involved in this strategy?

This is an interesting term – how "passive" should an investor be? Investors can be passive, though they should at least understand the projects and risk when they invest.

➢ How much money would people need to do what you do? How much training?

Lots and lots, in that order. Time to run the business is another big requirement amongst many others.

➢ What do you see as the main risks in property today, or what risks are you facing?

The usual risk of over leveraging and the changing market.

> **What steps if any are you taking to ensure a good future for your portfolio, especially considering the tax changes?**

Very low or no leveraging.

> **People often ask about TIME: How much time did you put in at the beginning, to get started? How much skill did you have?**

We've been growing this business since 2013. We have utilised skills gained throughout our careers, and trained and learned along the way. It takes a lot of our time and commitment. The skills we have accrued and developed vary greatly.

> **Regarding scaling up – do you have staff now, or would you like to in future?**

We're just starting to scale – watch this space!

> **How ambitious are you? What motivates you?**

I'm not sure the word ambitious fits? Most things motivate me, and a lot of it comes down to caring and sharing for and with others.

> **Do you combine what you do with other property strategies?**

A little, but that will change as time allows.

How well would you say your property strategy fits with other strategies and do you use a combination of strategies?

Well, in most respects, apart from time. I do expect that to change in time.

> **What would be your advice to others on combining or adding on strategies?**

Understand why you're considering new strategies, will they be complementary and/or will they lower your market risk? Do you want to scale up or out?

➢ **Can people use your services? Do you offer training, coaching or mentoring?**

Absolutely, just go to www.SimpleCrowdfunding.co.uk to find out more.

➢ **What would be your top tips for readers: what are the most important things they need to know?**

I've had a few people ask me how to get into property, and have the same answer each time.

Go to as many free property seminars as you can in 3/6 months and buy NOTHING! During that time you will work out who you want to work with and what strategy suits you.

Consider 'learn and invest' strategies where you get to be in a real deal and learn while possibly making a return!

Develop yourself, read (or listen) to self-development books as well as property books.

➢ **What are your thoughts on property taxation?**

Tax is very specific to an individual's situation, so speak to a good accountant or tax specialist.

➢ **Who inspires you? Are you into self-development? What writers or speakers do you like?**

Everyone is inspirational if you look (or listen) hard enough. ☺

If readers want to get in touch with you, where can they do that?

www.SimpleCrowdfunding.co.uk or Davin@SimpleCrowdfunding.co.uk

APPENDIX IV: Dave's Diary

 Here are some more excerpts from Dave's Diary over a typical monthly period. I hope this will help to give you some insights into the typical maintenance issues that commonly arise with buy-to-lets:

21st July: Bailiffs evicted the tenant at 23C. The tenant wasn't there when I arrived with the bailiffs. I changed the lock and gained lawful entry with the bailiffs. My gas engineer turned up and said the tenant was waiting round the back with others. I went 'round' and there she was with her mother, brother and friend. The brother shouted at me. They came in and took a suitcase of stuff. I later heard they were put in temporary accommodation locally by the council (as usually happens) – a cheap hotel.

I didn't start work at the property (other than changing two kitchen unit cupboard doors and changing the bathroom light for a LED light fitting) until the tenants got their act together to return and take all their stuff on 5th August. (The mother came back once before that to take food.)

21st July: That afternoon, I went to 3H and changed a single glazed window pane in the front door that the tenant's ex-partner had smashed. I got the glass from a local glazier for £55 – wire reinforced glass (the cheapest type) cut to size. Regulations state that glazing in doors has to be either toughened, reinforced or laminated.

I also got a quote for replacing some double glazing at the house. (Some has already been replaced.) The tenant had got a quote from Anglian for £4,500 but my guy quoted £3,500, which is for the three bedrooms and new doors front and back. (Yes, the door I just fixed had to be done urgently but does need replacing!)

8th August: Put up roller blind at 17B and stripped paper at 24C.

9th August: Craig came to help at 24C – he's a young guy who's related to one of my motorbike mates. Craig does painting which is a great help.

I paint stripped a couple of rows of tiles in the bathroom that had been painted over by tenants.

I ripped up carpet that needs changing on the landing and in bedrooms.

10th August: Finished paint stripping the bath tiles and put up curtain rails. I started glossing doors and Craig was there painting.

11th August: Ben the boiler man fitted a new boiler at 24C. Craig was also there painting.

12th August: I changed the lock at 7A as the tenant snapped their key off in the lock.

13th August: Angela and I went to 24C and mowed the lawn front and back and tidied the garden. I also did more gloss-work painting.

14th August: Fitted door stops and painted ceilings 24C. Craig painting.

15th August: Craig painting.

16th August: 24C painting including loft hatch; carpeted small bedroom.

2pm: Health and Safety visit / inspection at 48H,

17th August: Worked at 48H: Bled radiators, re-hung a window, replaced light switch, re-hung a door.

Radiators need bleeding sometimes as they get air bubbles which stops them from heating up as they should. They have a bleed valve which you can turn to let the air out to fix the problem. You then have to re-pressurise the boiler.

18th August: Angela at 24C – not Dave for 4 days, as doing motorbike training and test. Angela cleaned the bathroom and the floor in the inner and outer 'lobby' areas. Did some filling and painting of dog-scratched cladding in outer lobby area by back door.

19th August: Angela cleaned the kitchen including the floor and started to clean the laminate on the lounge floor until too tired to continue!

20th August: Angela painted the outside cladding and door, finished cleaning the lounge floor.

21st August: Angela rinsed the bath and cleaned the floor of the downstairs toilet.

PM: Dave showed the house to an ex-tenant who had contacted him at the weekend to enquire if anywhere available. They want to take the house. We still have to carpet the place, otherwise it's ready to rent. Job done!

This tenant has lived at 3 of our properties in the past! Her mum has also lived at another. Good tenant. We were getting rent £950 at this house but now will get £1,100.

22nd August: Went to fit lino 24C bathroom and noticed toilet pan was cracked, so bought a new toilet for £27 from Graham's (builders' merchants – national?), removed old loo and fitted new.

Re-pressurised the combi boiler at 6W. Looked at fallen tree 15B.

Fitted radiator back up that was falling off the wall at 15B. Open vented system, not pressurised. I loosened the pipes, so the radiator could swing onto my lap while I re-attached the brackets to the wall with new rawlplugs, then put radiator back up, secured and tightened the pipes back up.

21P: Started trying to fix the toilet that wasn't flushing. I decided it needed a new siphon.

Also went to 56H and changed the seal in their float valve in the toilet as it was very noisy.

23rd August: Changed the flush mechanism on the toilet at 21P. It leaked from around where the cistern joined the pan every time toilet was flushed, so I had to leave it un-flushable after 4 hours of unsuccessfully trying to fix it. Very frustrating. (Luckily there is a 2nd toilet in the house.)

24th August: 10–am: Damp survey at 56H. The man said the damp in the kitchen was caused by the washing machine leaking - which the tenants fitted themselves.

I also bled some radiators at the property that weren't heating up.

Went to see the guy fitting double glazing at 11B for me.

12 midday: Met Ben the plumber at 21P, for him to look at the toilet I couldn't fix. He couldn't detect what the problem was either.

25th August: Changed two existing power points /socket outlets at 14F that weren't working – plugs couldn't be inserted. (This is non-notifiable work.)

I also re-hung garden gate at 56H with a new piece of wood and new post.

26th August: Worked on 21P toilet for another two hours.

27th August: Day off for family event.

28th August: Met two builders at 56H to get quote for roof and brickwork that needs replacing on brick-built outbuilding/shed.

29th August: Fitted a new toilet at 21P. When I removed the old toilet, I found out that the problem we hadn't been able to identify was that a part of the diaphragm from the old siphon had broken off and got stuck in the waterways obstructing the flush and causing a leak from where the cistern joins the pan. The new toilet being a close coupled type was £50 from B&Q. You can't buy just the pan for this type. I didn't need a new cistern but had to buy a whole set.

I also met a tree surgeon at 15B for a quote to remove a tree after part of it broke away and fell onto the neighbour's house – luckily causing no damage.

Then went to remove a TV aerial at 56H as it was beginning to be unstable and not used anyway.

30th August: I changed the TV aerial socket on the wall at 18T; replaced an electric shower at 6W and started fitting carpets at 24C; and met an electrician at 56H about an electrical safety survey. He said it needs RCDs fitted in the fuse-box and it'll cost £320 to change the fuse-box and do the electrical test, which he'll come back to do.

31st August: The tenant at 6D started moving out. I finished fitting new carpets at24C.

I bought special fixings for the doorframe at 56H where their special-needs son kept slamming the door, causing the plaster to fall off the walls. I got the fixings from Bryant Fixings! Expanding type that gives a stronger hold.

1st September: Fitted new door lock at 6D as her drunken mother had tried to occupy the place and was messing with the tenant's belongings.

2nd – 3rd September: Weekend off, although me and Angela went to look at a few properties. Angela saw 6D for first time after tenant moved out. We also went to check on 6C which is sold (grass growing!), 15B where the tree fell; and Angela saw carpets that I fitted at 24C which is now ready for tenant to move in.

4th September: I had to adjust the new lock at 6D after the tenant's mother had tried to break back in.

Went to see the double-glazing man fitting windows at 3H.

Accepted quote for shed roof and brickwork at 56H.

Met plasterer at 56H. He quoted £200 for patches that need re-plastering in two rooms.

5th September: Tree got cut down at 15B and I went to watch.

I also visited the double-glazing man again at 3H.

6th September: Went back to 15B to repair three loose bricks that I noticed had come away from the house wall. I got some cement and fixed them back in! I also put poison on the tree stump after it was cut down.

Mowed the lawn at a small block of 6 flats where we own two, and the owners have formed a management committee, and self-manage the communal areas.

7th September: Replaced shed door 56H. Door from Magnets £50, ledged & braced door, 33" wide plus £5 pair of hinges.

Signed up 24C AST.

Met Steve at 6D to quote for new kitchen and bathroom.

32S looked at shower; pressed reset button on RCD.

8th September: Finished shed door at 56H – it needed planning.

Had new fuse-box and electrical test at 56H.

Dropped off keys for 23S/H where the sale completed today.

4B: Changed the thermostat on the emergency heater which kept tripping (I had one in stock).

Looked at 2N where the cladding needs replacing.

APPENDIX V: Author's Booklist

This booklist is provided for general purposes and includes the books and audiobooks I have read that may be of interest. I have put the books into various categories. Dates are included in some cases, but not in the health and longevity section or the classic books that I read years ago, where the dates of publication are of little relevance:

Three Most Recently Read Books:

High Performance Habits (How Extraordinary People Become that Way), Brendon Burchard (Sept 2017)

Master Your Time, Master Your Life, Brian Tracy (Oct 2017)

The Five Second Rule, Mel Robbins (Mar 2017)

Property Related Books:

The Complete Guide to Property Investing Success, Angela Bryant (Dec 2008)

Complete HMO Property Success, Nick Fox (Jan 2016)

HMO Landlord Rules, C J Haliburton (Jan 2015)

Property Sourcing Compliance: Keeping You on The Right Side of the Law, Tina Walsh (Sept 2017)

Rent-to-Rent Getting Started Guide, Jacquie Edwards (June 2017)

Simple Crowdfunding, Davin and Atuksha Poonwassie (Sept 2015)

The Absolute Essence of Inheritance Tax Planning, Steve Parnham (2017)

Recent Business and Mindset Books:

Strategic Planning Kit for Dummies (2nd edition), Erica Olsen (Nov 2011)

The 10 Times Rule: The Only Difference Between Success and Failure, Grant Cardone (May 2011)

The Millionaire Fastlane, MJ DeMarco (Dec 2011)

How Rich People Think, Steve Siebold (July 2010)

The Power of Habit, Charles Duhigg (Feb 2013)

The Miracle of Self-Discipline, Brian Tracy (May 2010)

The Thoughtful Leader, Mindy Gibbins-Klein (Jan 2015)

Life Leverage, Rob Moore (June 2016)

Uncommon Sense, Mark Homer (Jan 2017)

How to Write Your Book Without the Fuss, Lucy Mc Carraher, Joe Gregory (Aug 2015)

Psychology and General Mindset Books:

Metamorphosis, Polly Morland (May 2017)

30 Days: Change Your Habits, Change Your Life, Marc Reklau (Aug 2014)

The New Year's Resolution Handbook, David Hyner (Dec 2015)

The Pleasure Trap, Douglas J Lisle (Mar 2006)

The Willpower Instinct, Kelly McGonigal (Dec 2013)

Breaking the Habit of Being Yourself, Dr Joe Dispenza (Mar 2012)

It's All In Your Mind, Lindsey Sharratt (Nov 2015)

The Chimp Paradox, Prof Steve Peters (Jan 2012)

101 Power Thoughts for Life, Louise L Hay (Aug 2004)

Health, Longevity and Running Books:

Marathon and Half Marathon, Sam Murphy

The Spectrum, Dean Ornish

The 10 Secrets of Healthy Ageing, Patrick Holford

Loving Yourself to Great Health, Louise Hay

Optimum Nutrition Made Easy, Patrick Holford

Spring Chicken, Bill Gifford

Healthy at 100, John Robbins

The Fast Diet, Dr Michael Mosley

Living to 100, Perls & Silver

Prime-Time Health, William Sears

Lifelong Running, Heidrich

Older, Faster, Stronger, Margaret Webb

The Blue Zones Solution, Dan Buettner

Summary of How Not to Die, Michael Greger with Gene Stone

Run Yourself Fit, Christina MacDonald

More Books that Have Influenced Me:

How to Become a Millionaire, Jim Slater & Tom Stevenson

Manifest Your Destiny, Wayne Dyer

Awakening the Entrepreneur Within, Michael E Gerber

Cracking the Millionaire Code, Mark Victor Hansen & Robert G Allen

The Charge, Brendon Burchard

Rule # 1, Phil Town

Building Wealth, Russ Whitney

Think Yourself Rich, Sharon Maxwell Magnus

The Soul Millionaire, David J Scarlett

Cashflow Quadrant, Robert Kiyosaki

Rich Dad, Poor Dad, Robert Kiyosaki

The Power of Intention, Wayne Dyer

Wishes Fulfilled, Wayne Dyer

Getting Rich Your Own Way, Brian Tracy

Manifesting Change, Mike Dooley

7 Strategies for Wealth & Happiness, Jim Rohn

Billionaire in Training, Bradley J Sugars

Re-invention, Brian Tracy

The E-Myth Revisited, Michael Gerber

The Millionaire Mind, Thomas J Stanley

How to Get Rich, Felix Dennis

Secrets of the Millionaire Mind, T Harv Eker

Screw it, Let's Do It, Richard Branson

Unlimited Power, Anthony Robbins

How To Be Rich, J Paul Getty

Multiple Streams of Income, Robert G Allen

Maximum Achievement, Brian Tracy

The Millionaire Next Door, Thomas J Stanley, William D Danko

Awaken the Giant Within, Anthony Robbins

The Buy-to-Let Bible, Ajay Ahuja

Buying Bargains at Property Auction, Howard R Gooddie

The New No-Nonsense Landlord, Jorgensen

Time Power, Brian Tracy

Driven, Lawrence Nohria

Buying to Rent, Nick Rampley-Sturgeon

The Snowball, Warren Buffett, and *The Business of Life*, Alice Schroeder

The Small Business Start-Up Workbook, Cheryl D Rickman

The Real Deal, James Caan

The Power of Focus, Jack Canfield, Mark Victor Hansen, Les Hewitt

Dragons or Angels: An Unofficial Guide to Dragons Den & Bus. Investment, Modwenna Rees-Mogg

Think and Grow Rich, Napoleon Hill

Unfair Advantage, Robert Kiyosaki

E-Myth Mastery, Michael E Gerber

Retire Young, Retire Rich, Robert Kiyosaki

OPM – Other People's Money, 'Rich Dad's Advisors', Michael A Lechter

Rich Dad's Guide to Investing, Robert Kiyosaki

Rich Kid, Smart Kid, Robert Kiyosaki

The 80 / 20 Principle, Richard Koch

Find Your Lightbulb, Mike Harris

As A Man Thinketh, James Allen

The Master-Key To Riches, Napoleon Hill

Who Moved My Cheese? Dr Spencer Johnson

The Elephant and the Flea, Charles Handy

The Beermat Entrepreneur, Mike Southon & Chris West

The Angel Inside, Chris Widener

Public Speaking, Collins

How to Delegate, Robert Heller

Eat That Frog! Brian Tracy

Kiss That Frog! Brian Tracy & Christina Tracy Stein

What to Say When You Talk to Yourself, Shad Helmstetter

Think and Grow Rich Ever Day: 365 Days of Success, Napoleon Hill

The Magic, Rhonda Byrne

Feel the Fear and Beyond, Susan Jeffers

Fearless Living, Rhonda Britten

The Treasury of Quotes, Jim Rohn

Little Voice Mastery, Blair Singer

Instant Systems, Bradley J Sugars

Instant Referrals, Bradley J Sugars

Instant Repeat Business, Bradley J Sugars

Instant Profit, Bradley J Sugars

Instant Cashflow, Bradley J Sugars

House Dividing, Paul Hymers

How to Avoid Inheritance Tax, Carl Bayley

Speed Wealth, T Harv Eker

Twelve Pillars, Jim Rohn & Chris Widener

Home Extensions, Paul Hymers

It's Only Too Late if You Don't Start Now (How to create your 2nd life after 40), Barbara Sher

Home Extensions: Planning, Managing & Completing Your Extension, Laurie Williamson

The Millionaire Real Estate Mindset, Russ Whitney

See You at the Top, Zig Ziglar

About the Author

Angela Bryant lives in Sussex with her husband Dave, and has been a property investor since 1995, building a portfolio of over 100 properties, with a total value of £15,000,000 and several million in equity. She is the author of **The Complete Guide to Property Investing Success**.

Angela works on strategic planning, while Dave focuses on property maintenance and dealing with tenants. She also does admin and accounts and manages the non-local properties, as well as helping with refurbishments. Angela and Dave do not directly employ anyone but work with tradesmen and professionals as required. Additionally, they manage properties for one of Angela's brothers.

Having been involved in a few developments with brother Antony that all turned out well, Angela has been encouraged to shift focus more towards development, and the three biggest projects are described in Chapter 8.

Personal background:

- Married to Dave since the age of 21.

- Three grown-up children: Sophie, 28, Chris 24 and Matt 21.

- Angela has a degree in Psychology and Dave in Mechanical Engineering.

- She also enjoys running, having recently taken part in the Brighton half marathon.

Property investing background:

- First BTL property purchased in 1995, the value of which has risen fivefold from £33,000 to £165,000, while the whole portfolio has grown by five thousand times from this first seed.

- Angela gave up full-time work in 1989 and began planning the family's financial future in property.

- Dave gave up paid employment in March 2003 by which time they had 27 properties.

- Built a property portfolio of 100 properties, locally self-managed, as well as having non-local properties.

- Focused on various strategies over time, with the portfolio providing a solid foundation.

Printed in Great Britain
by Amazon